THIS BOOK BELONGS TO

I0508174

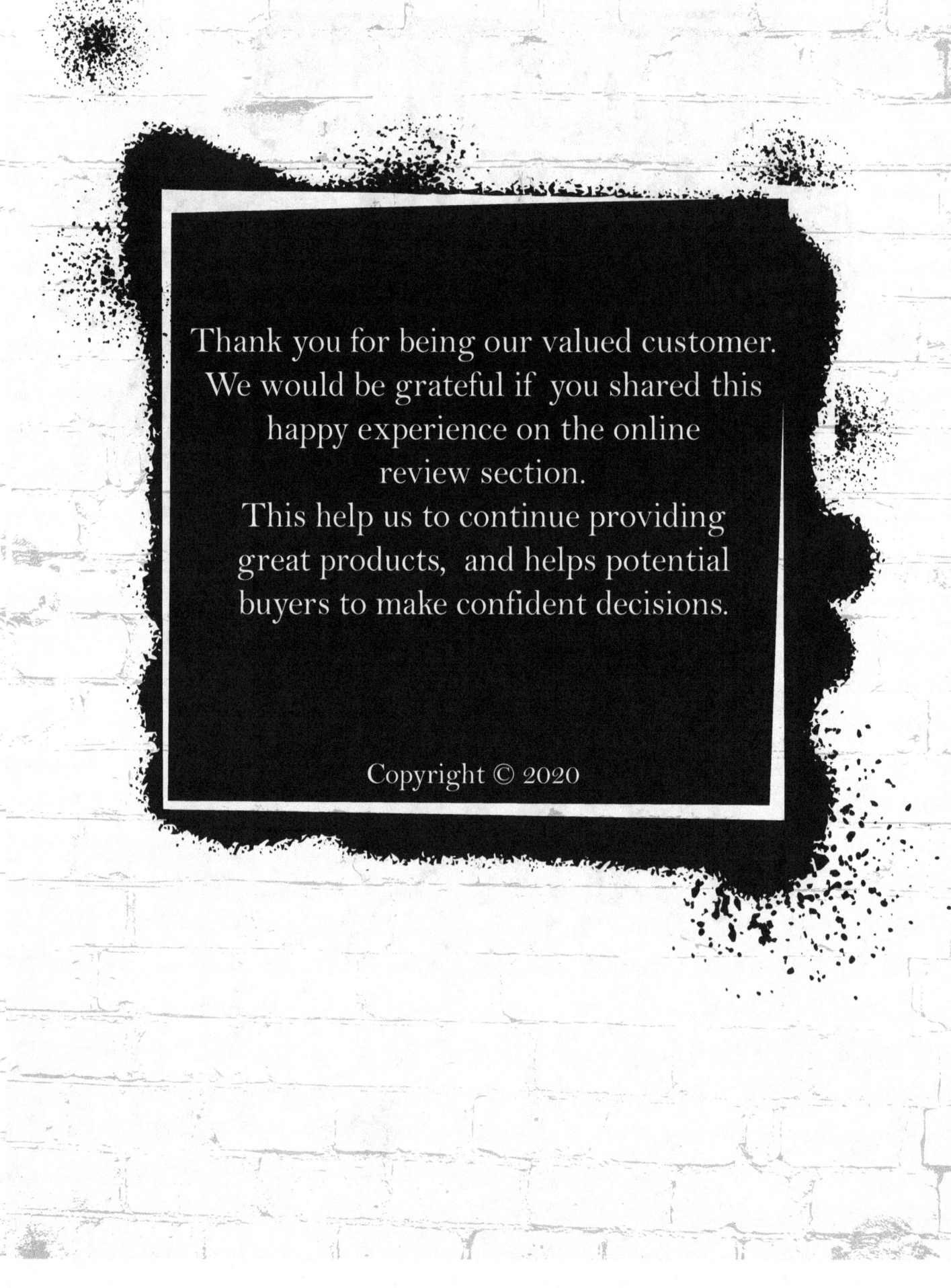

Thank you for being our valued customer.
We would be grateful if you shared this happy experience on the online review section.
This help us to continue providing great products, and helps potential buyers to make confident decisions.

Copyright © 2020

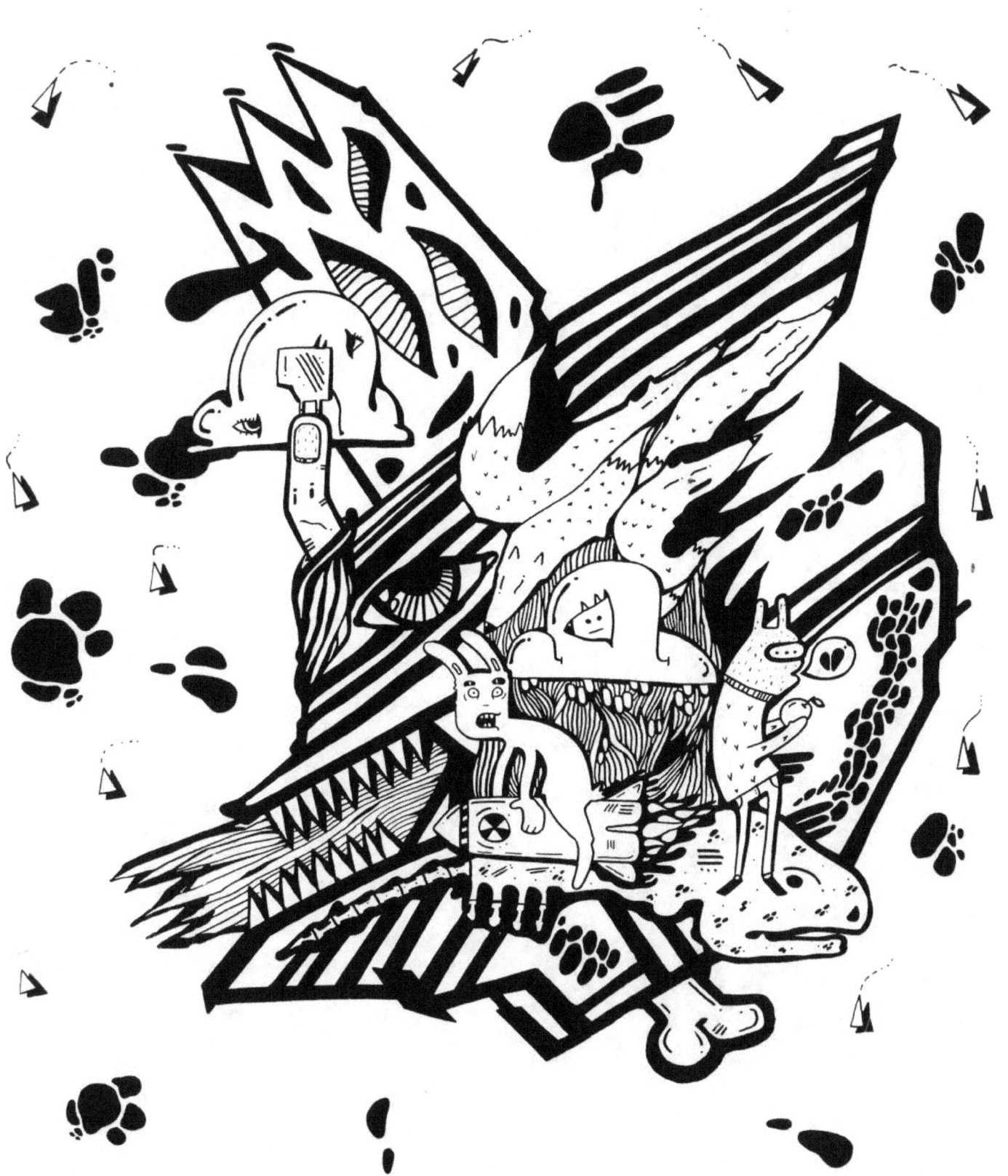

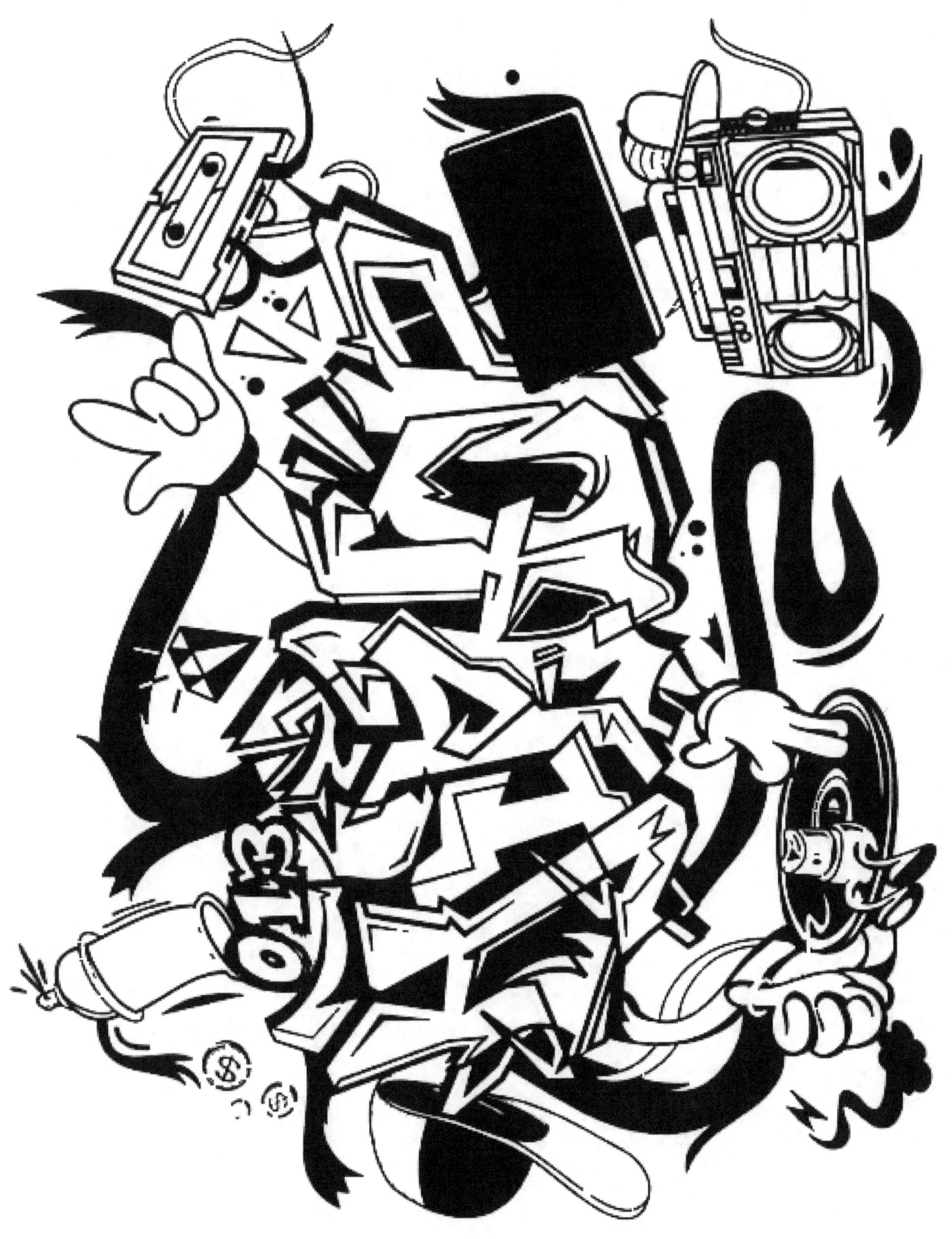

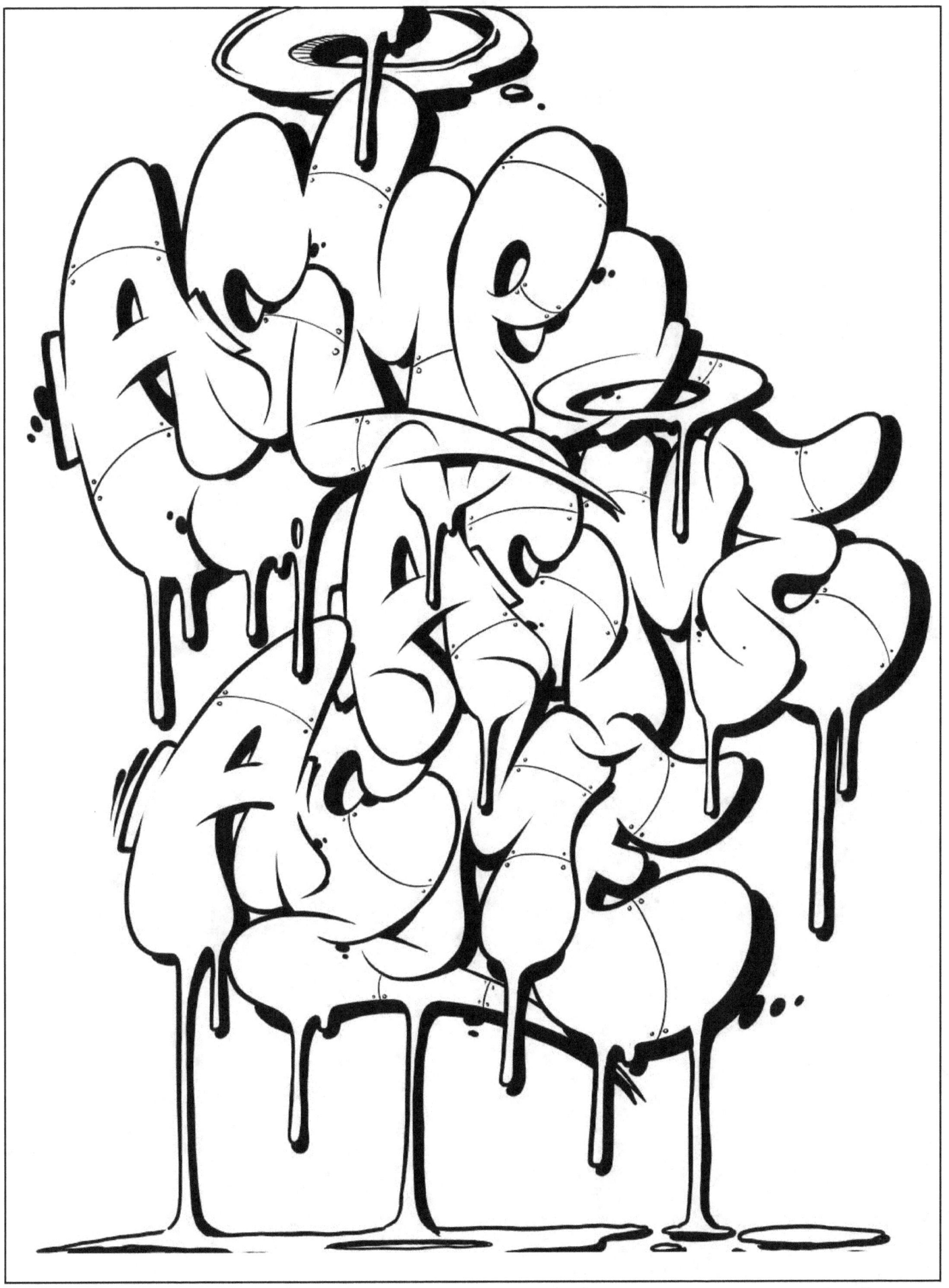

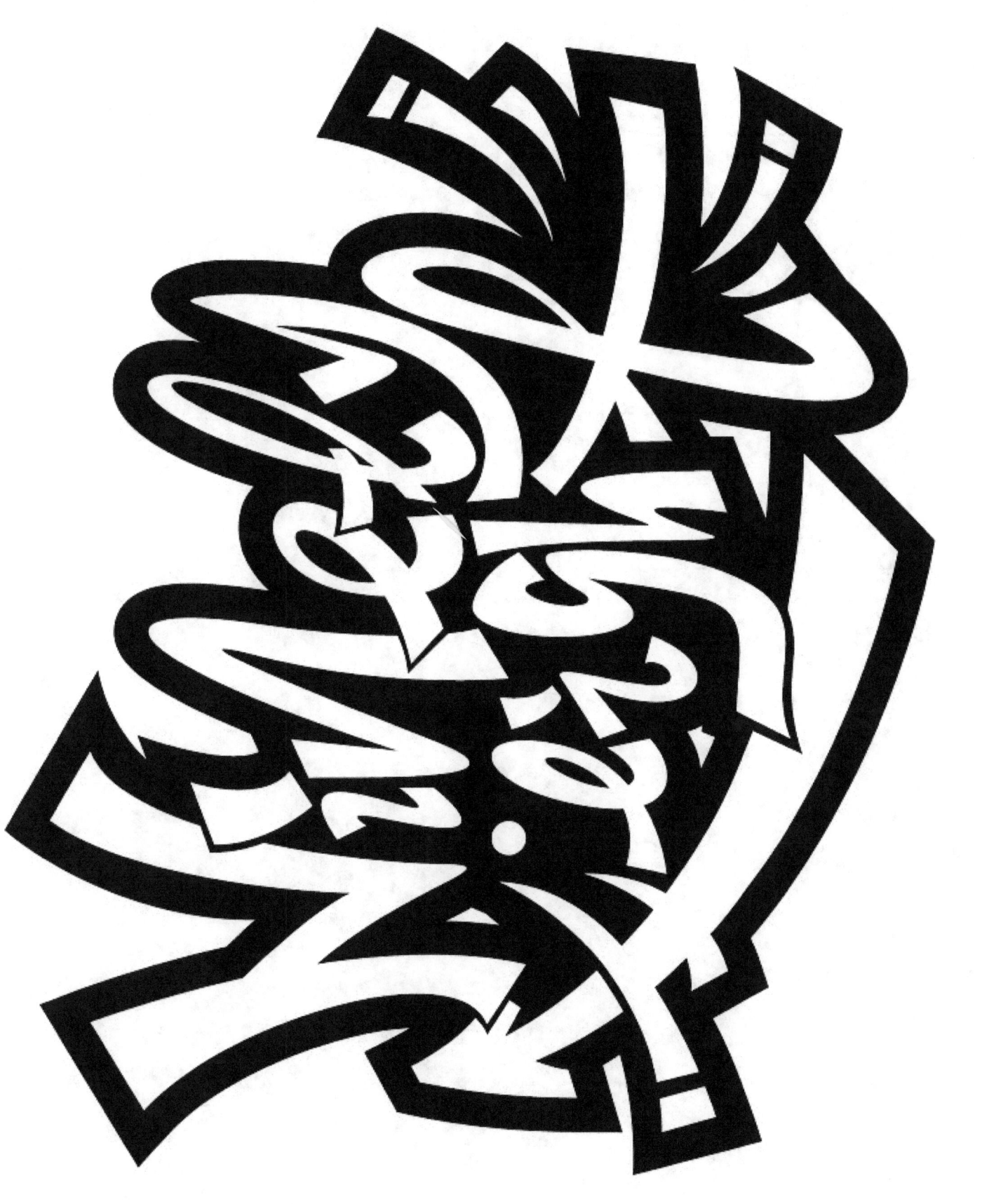

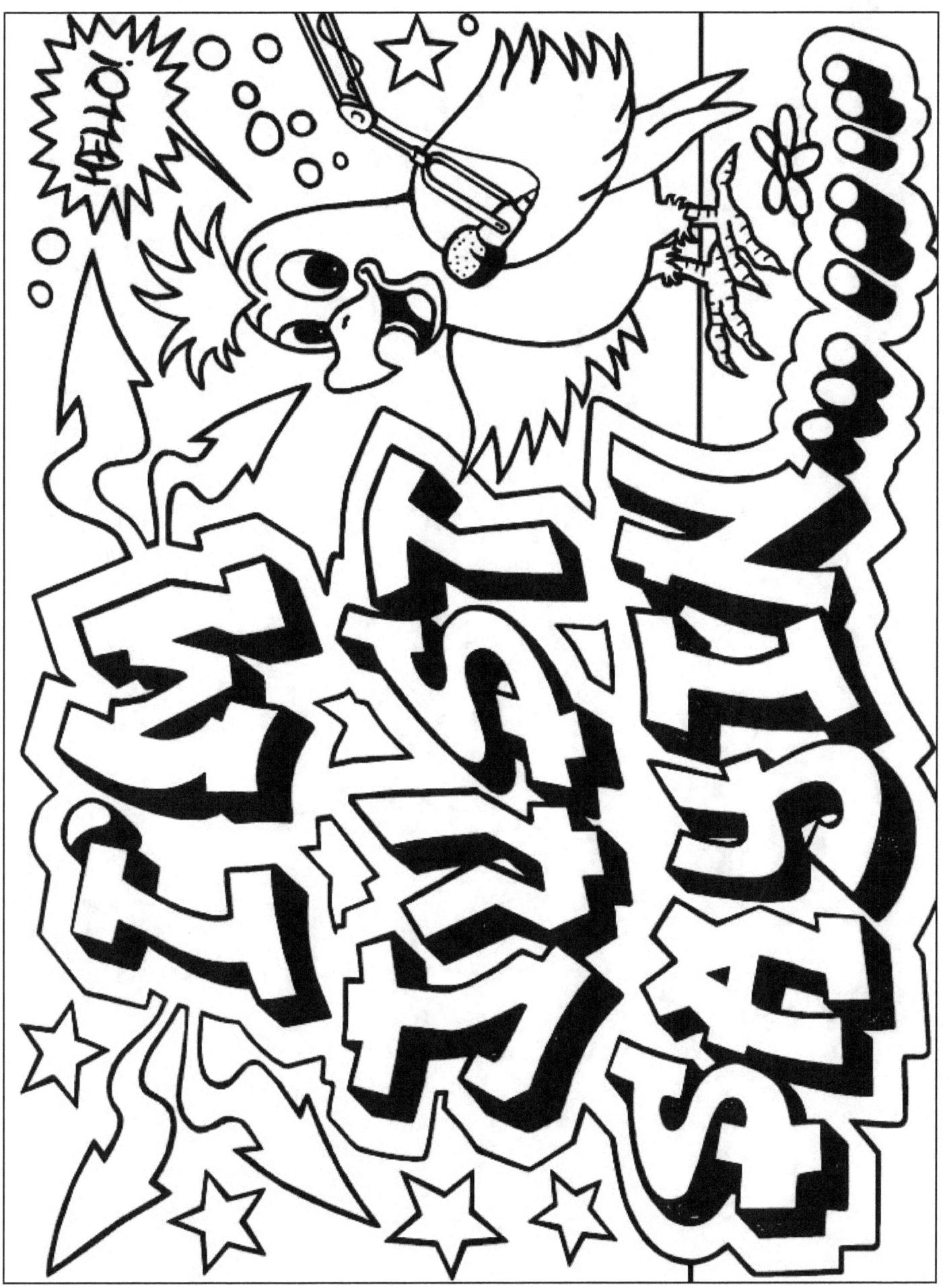

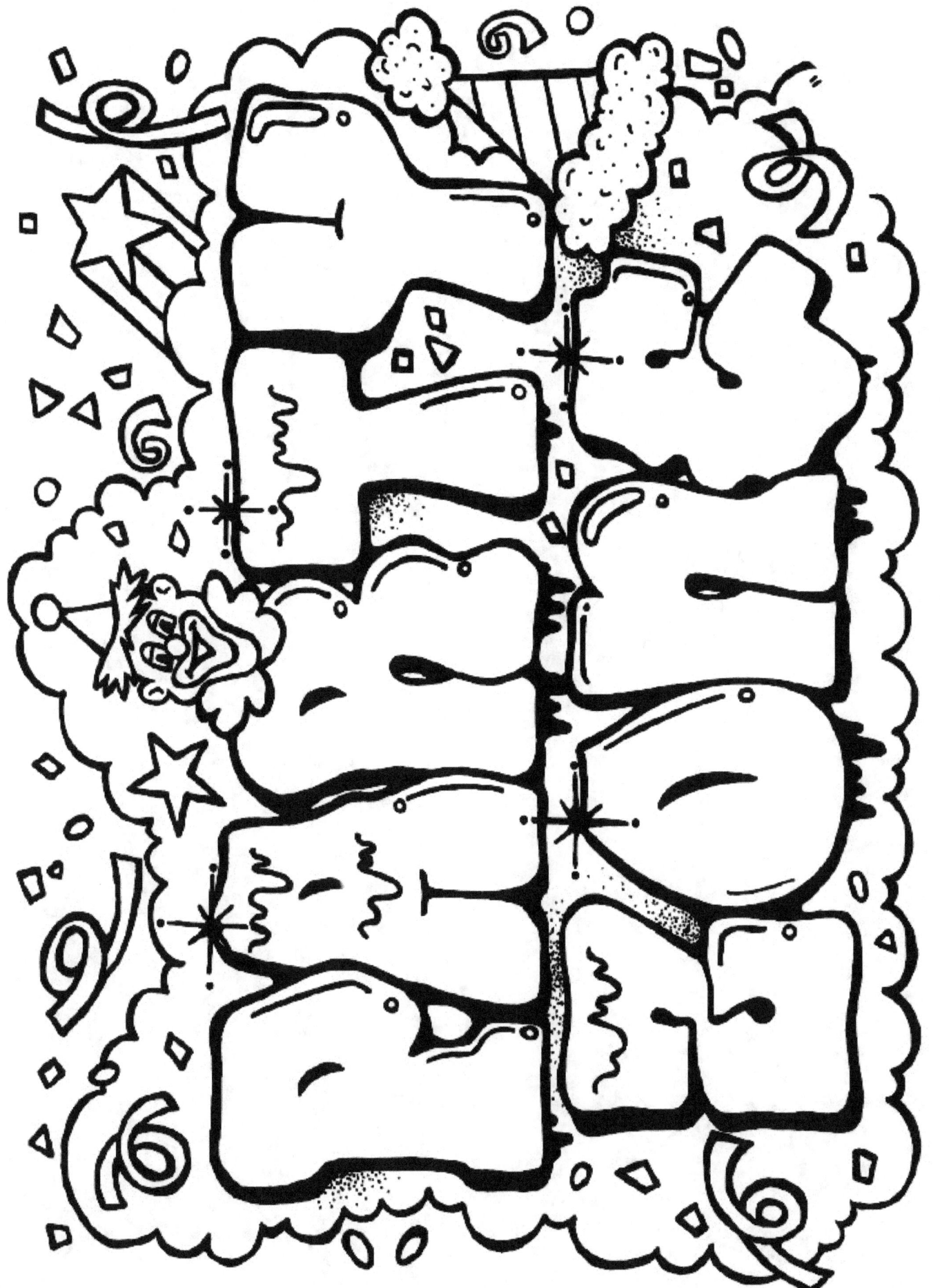

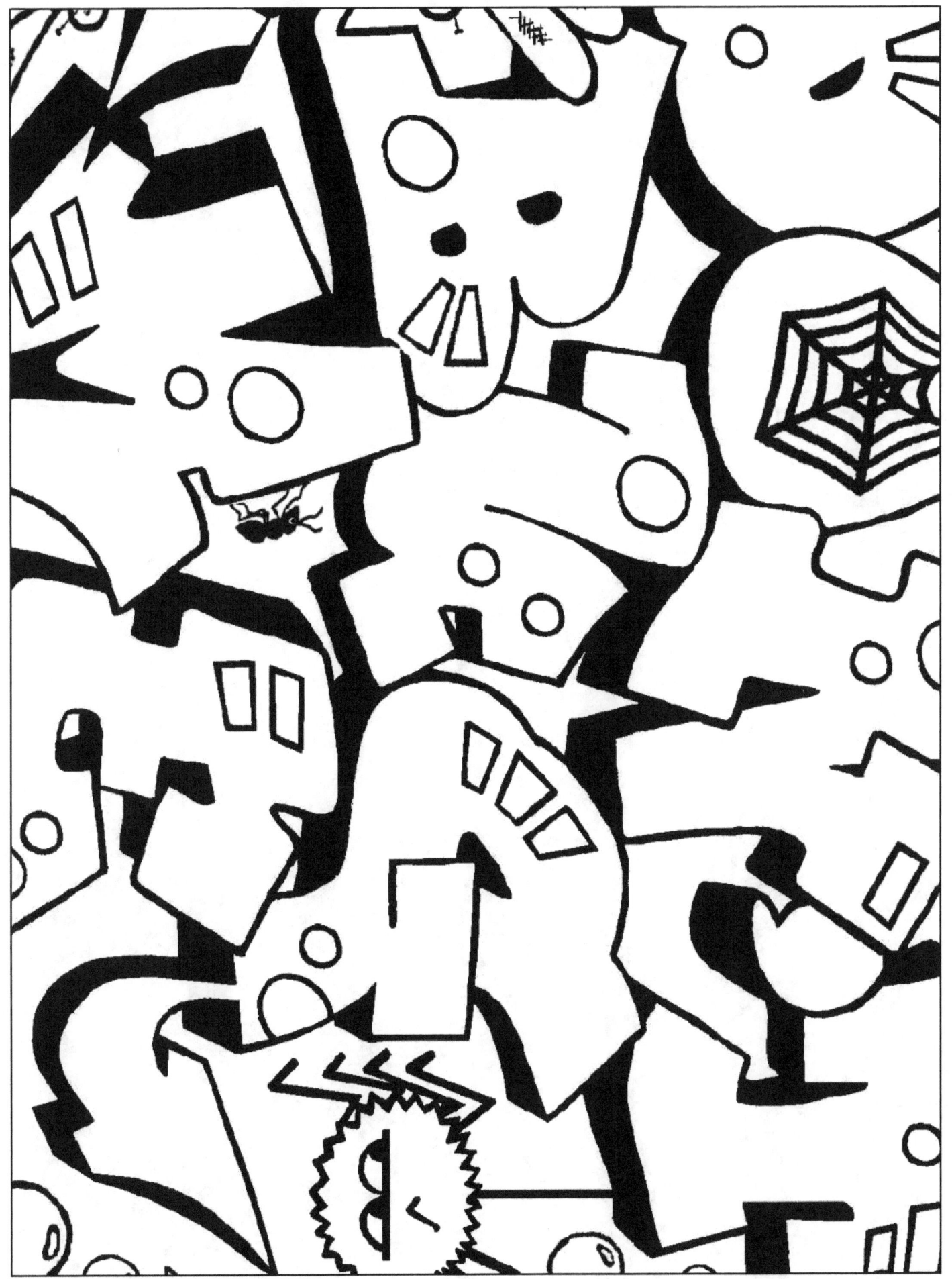

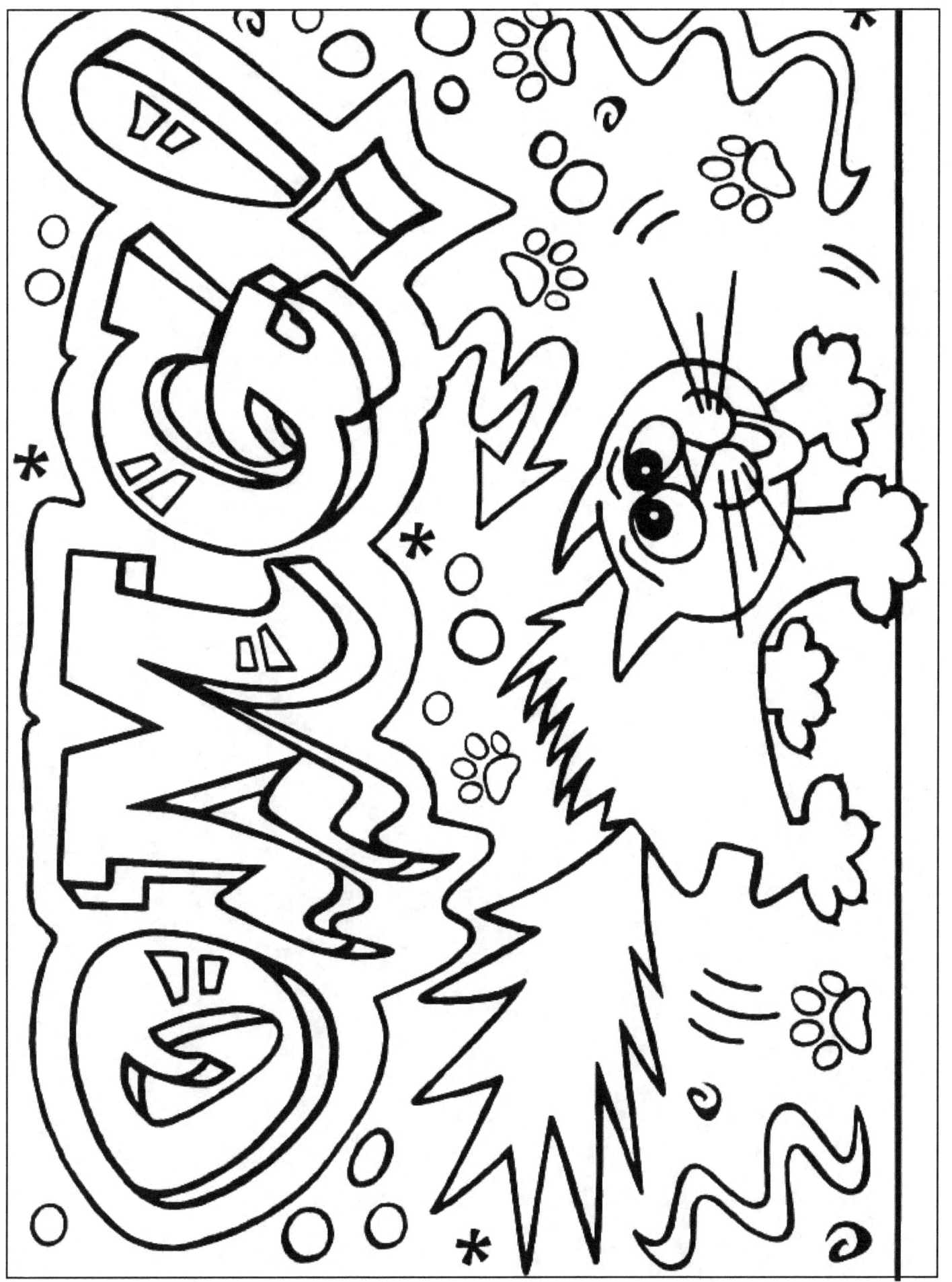

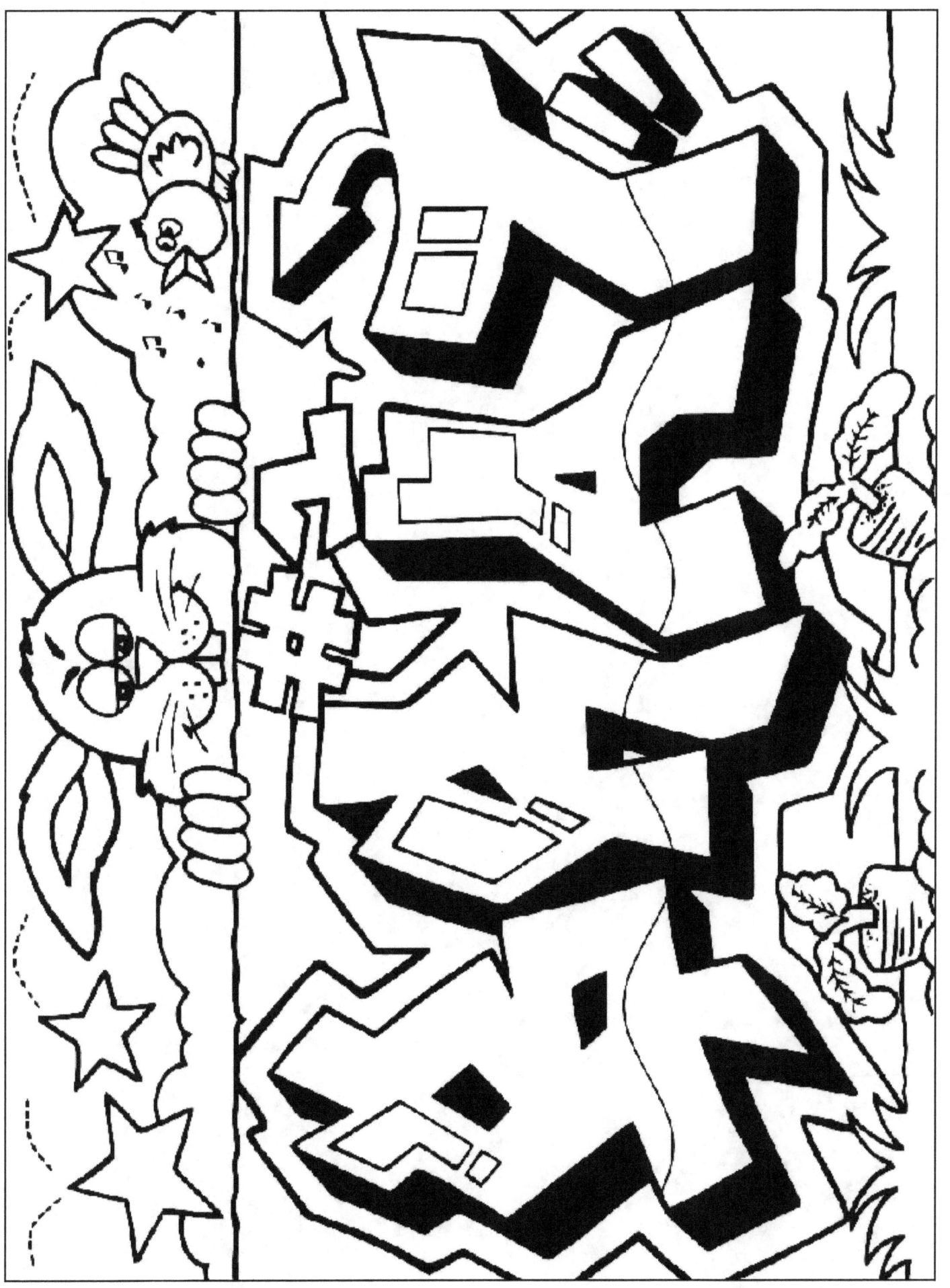

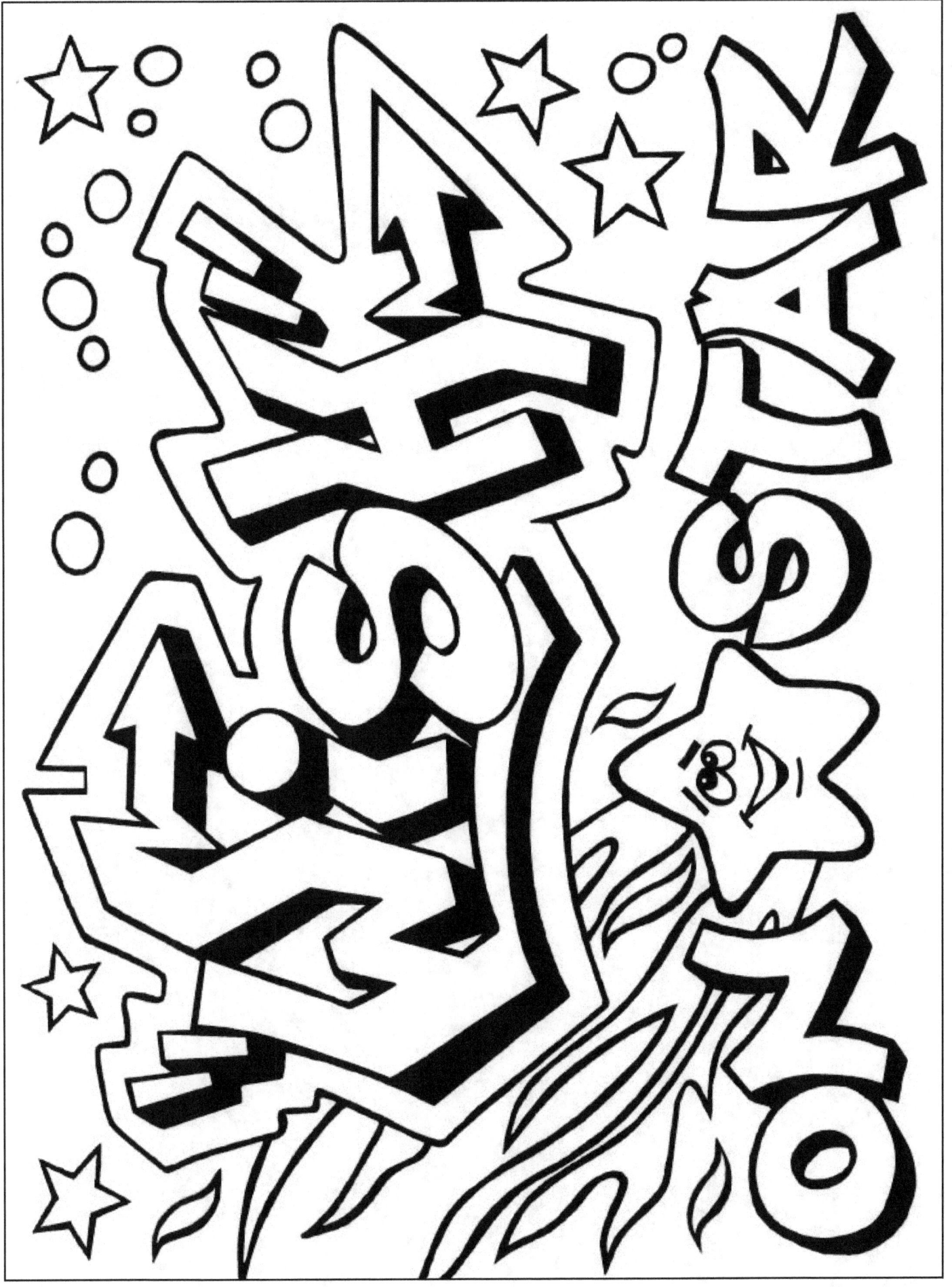

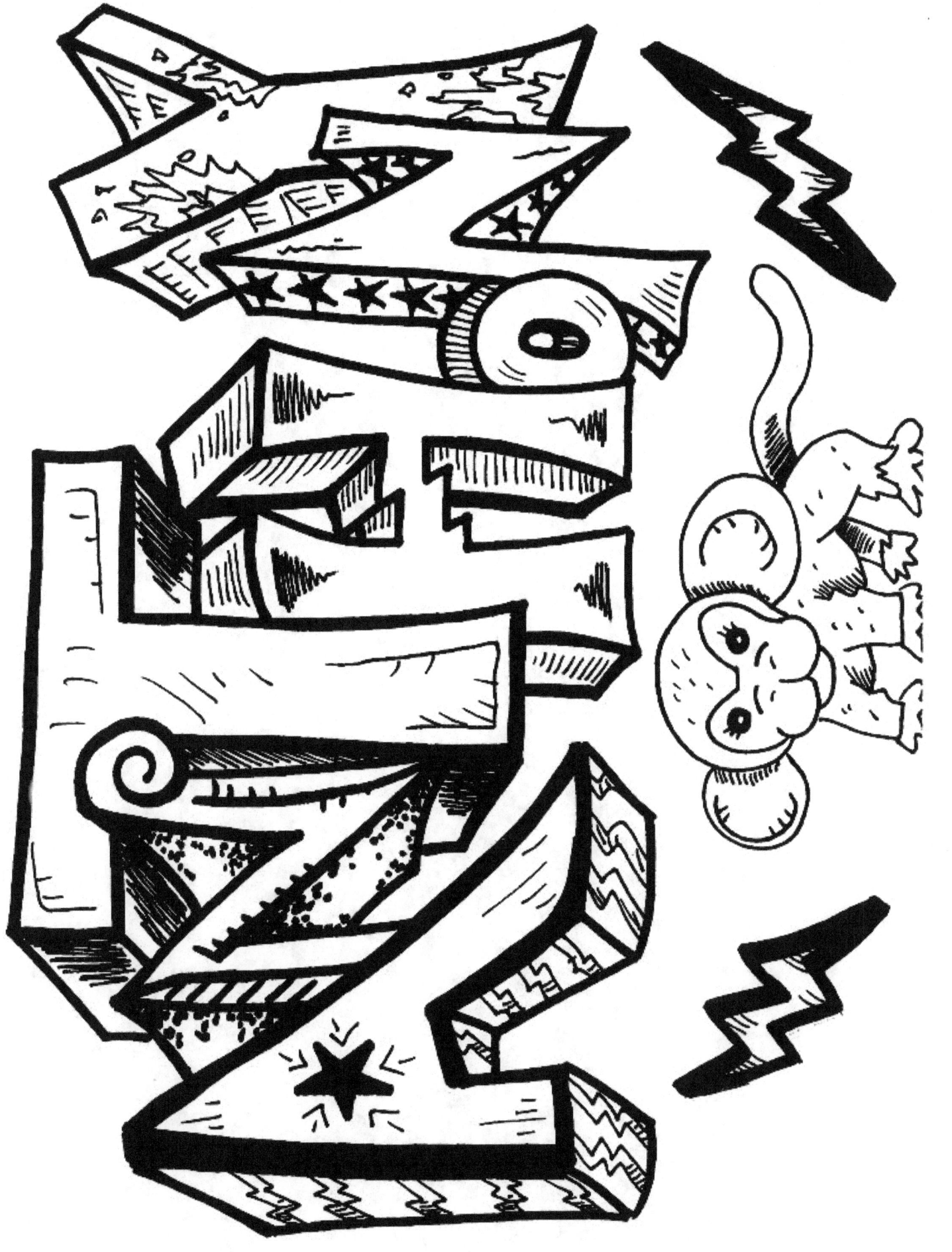

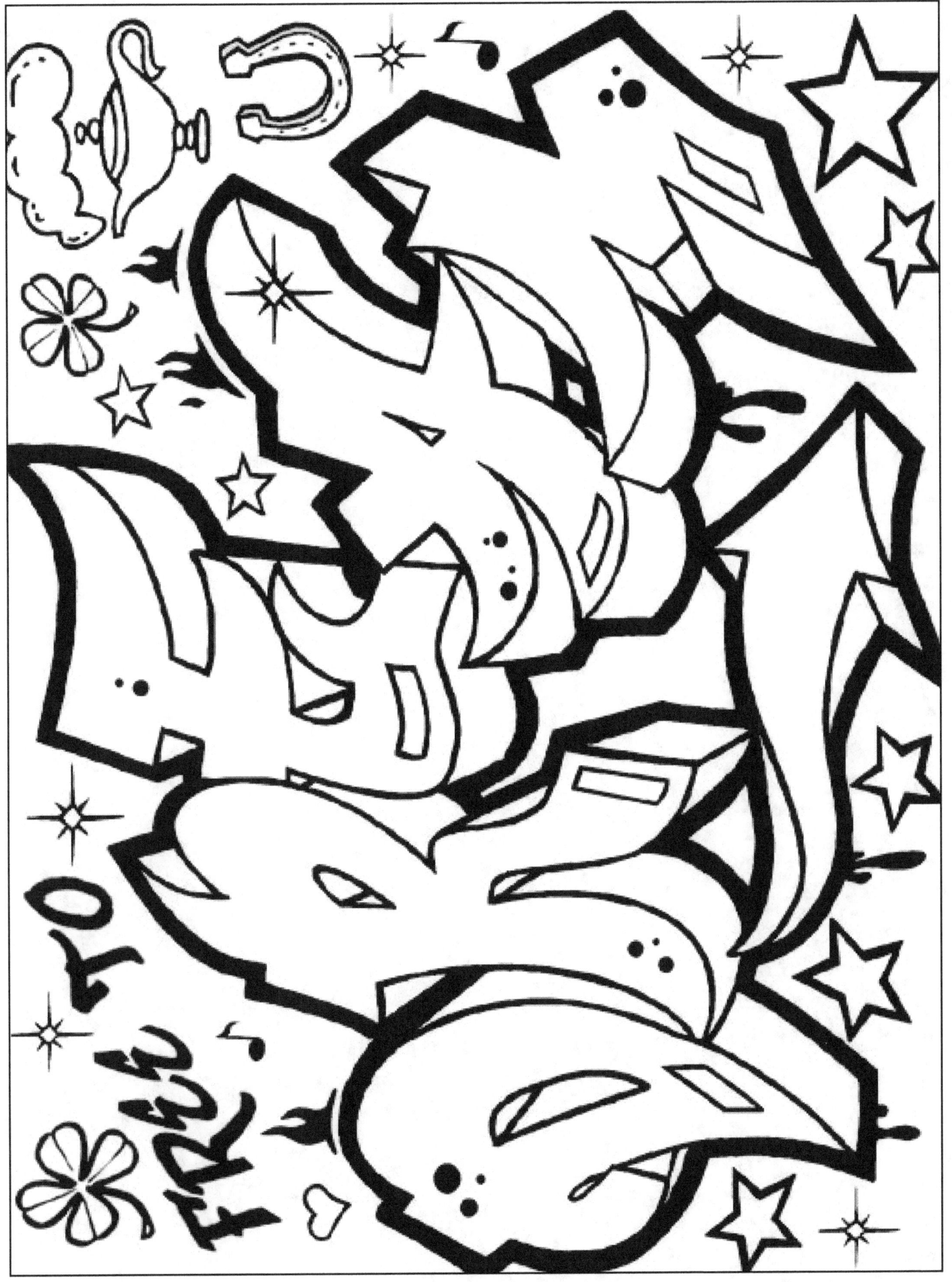

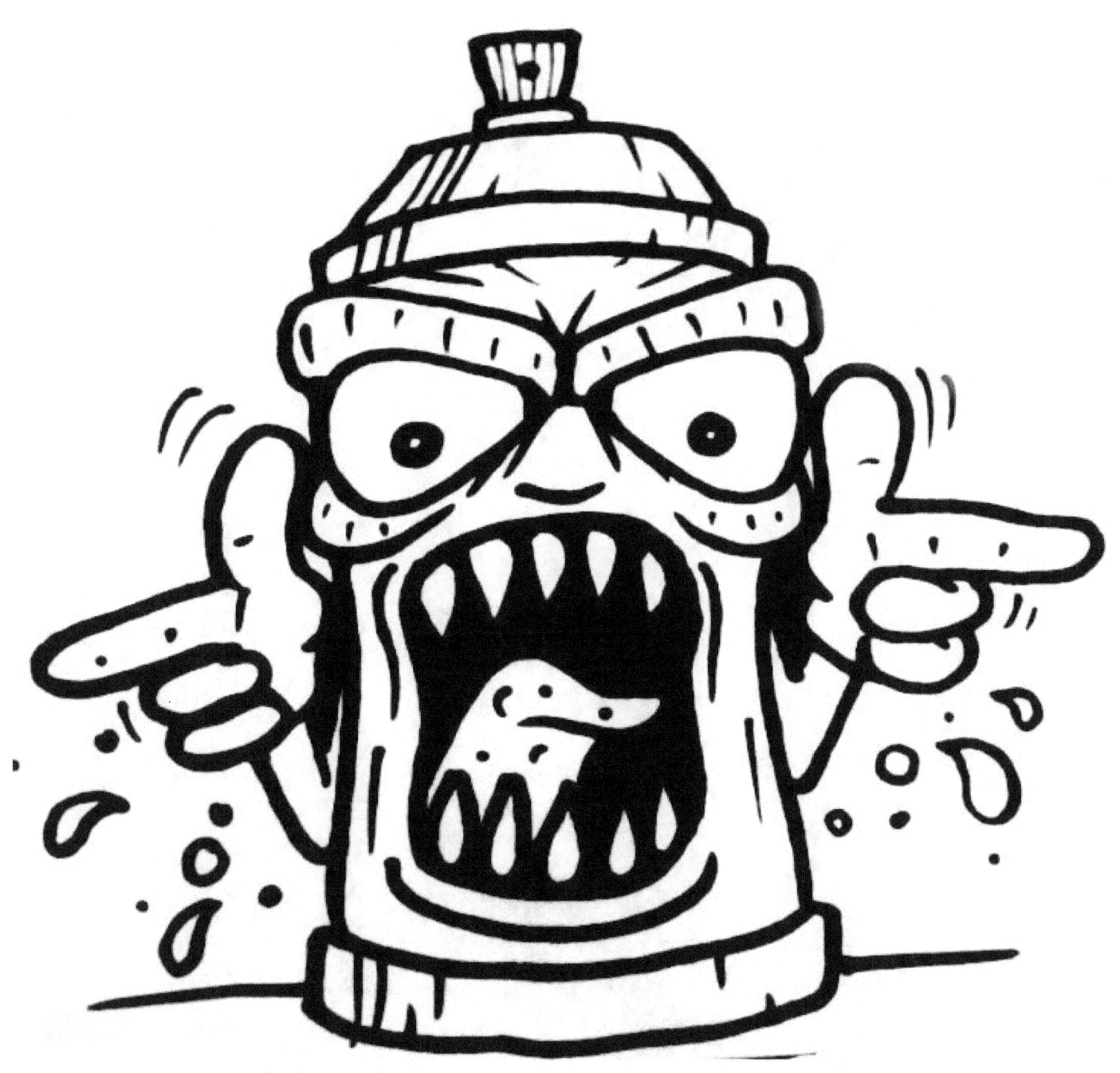

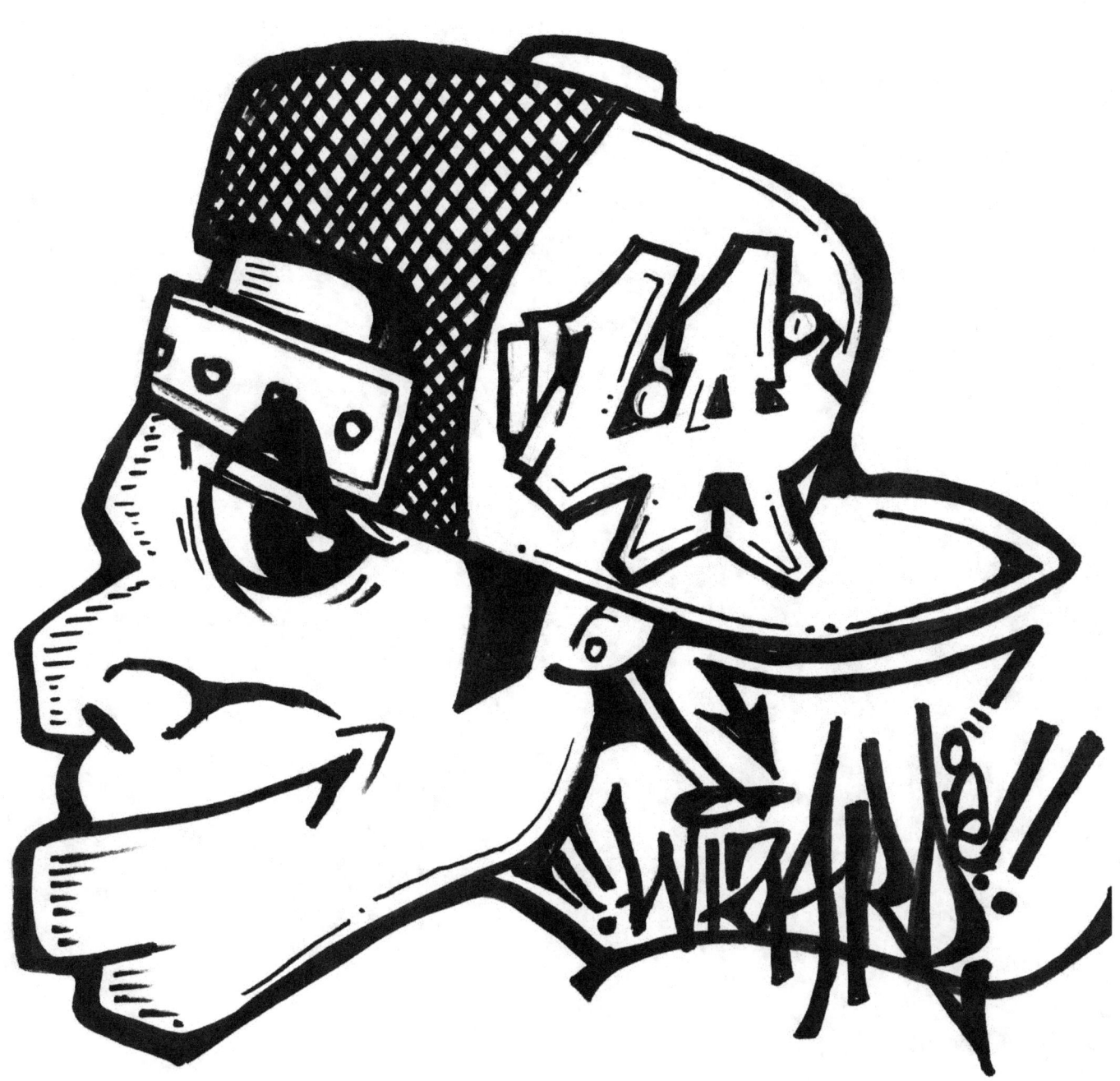

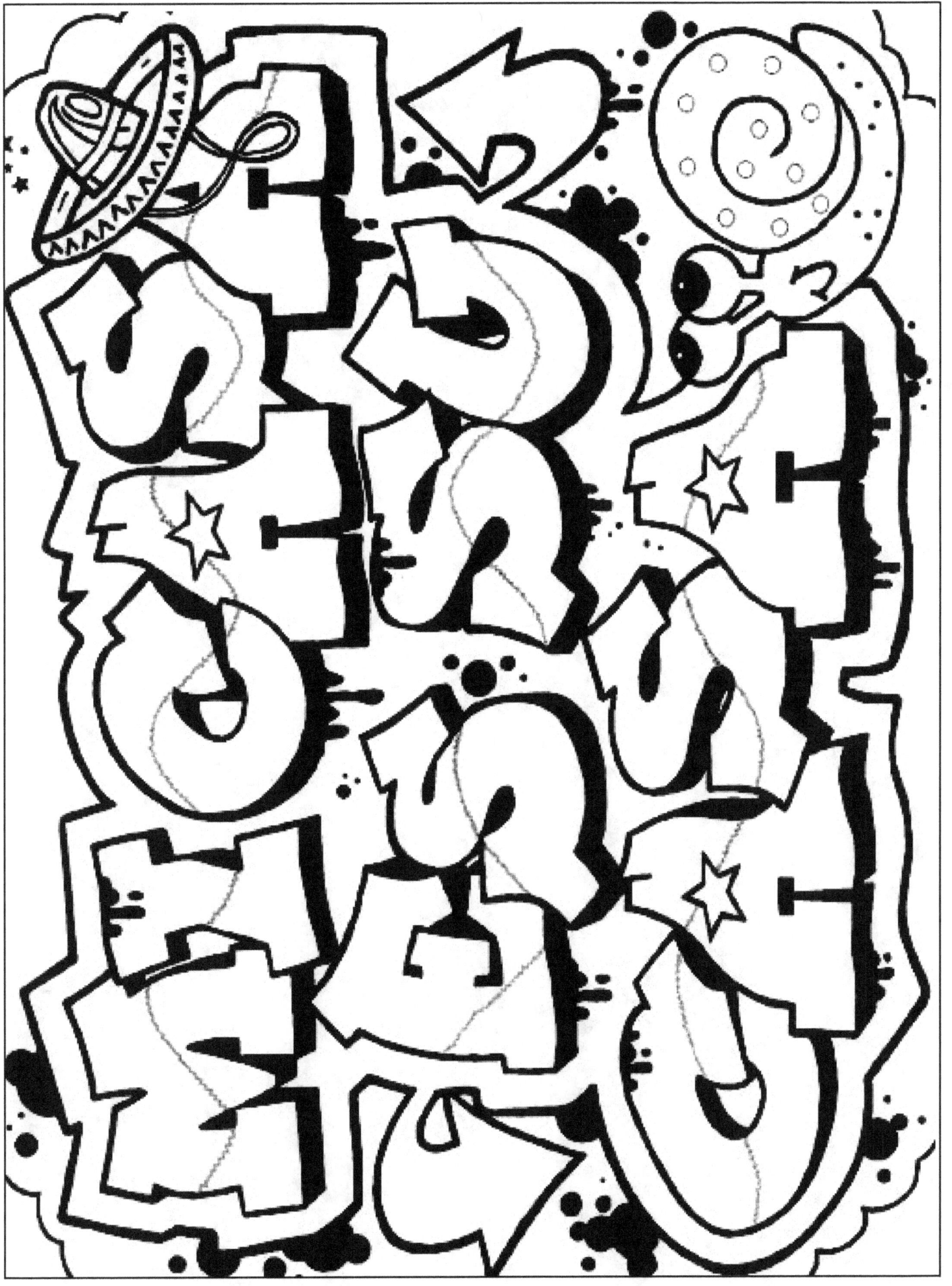

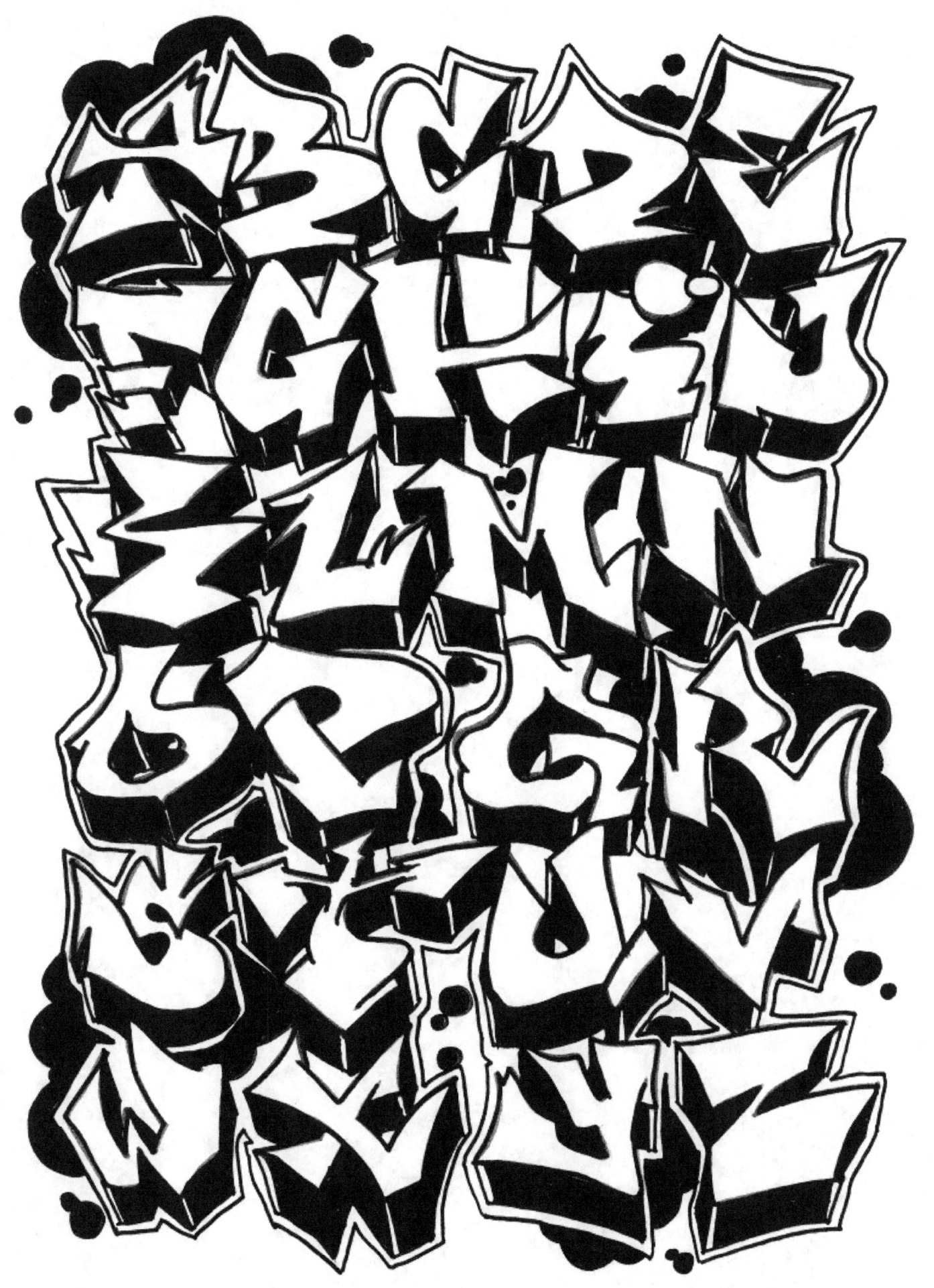

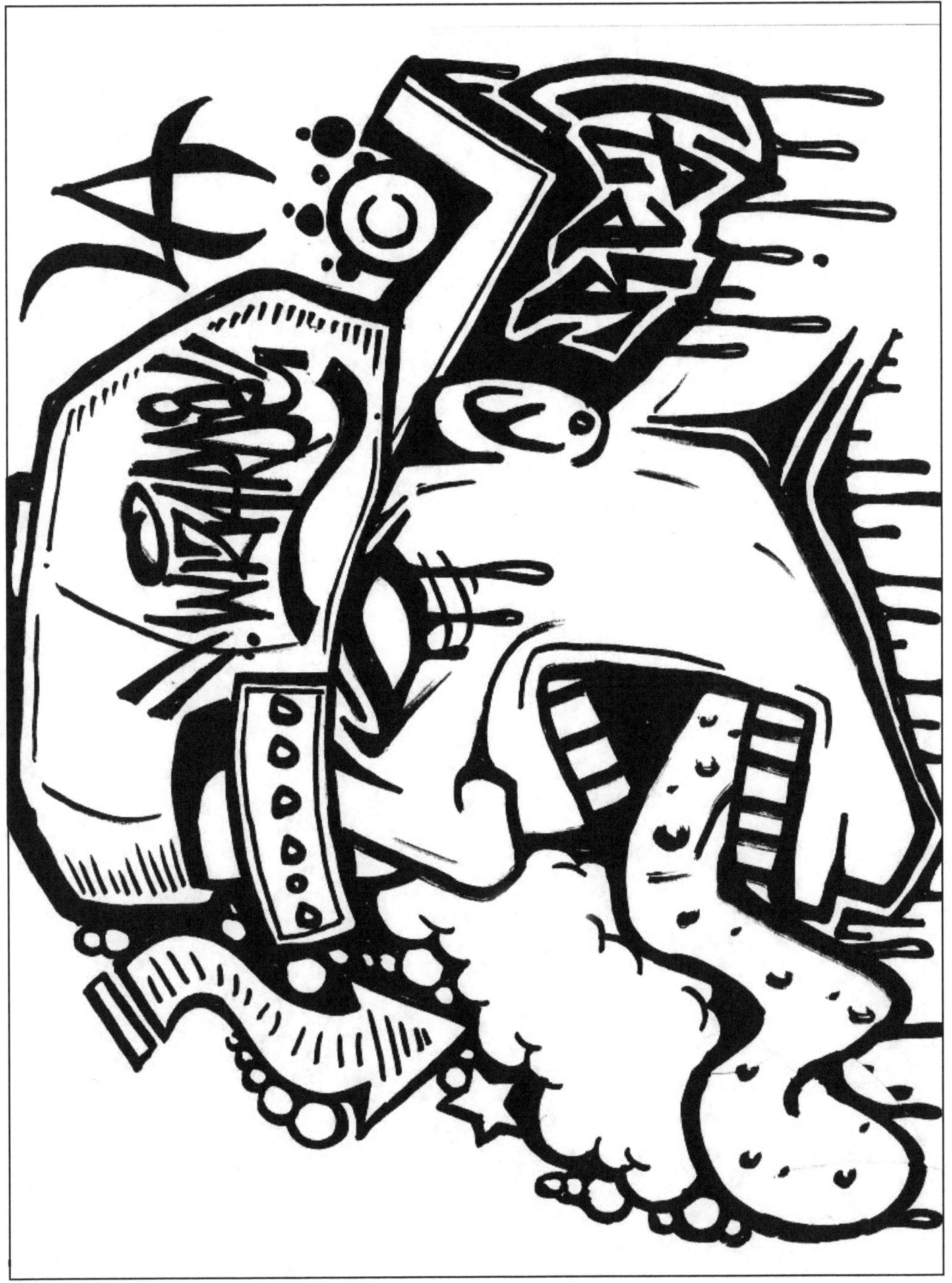

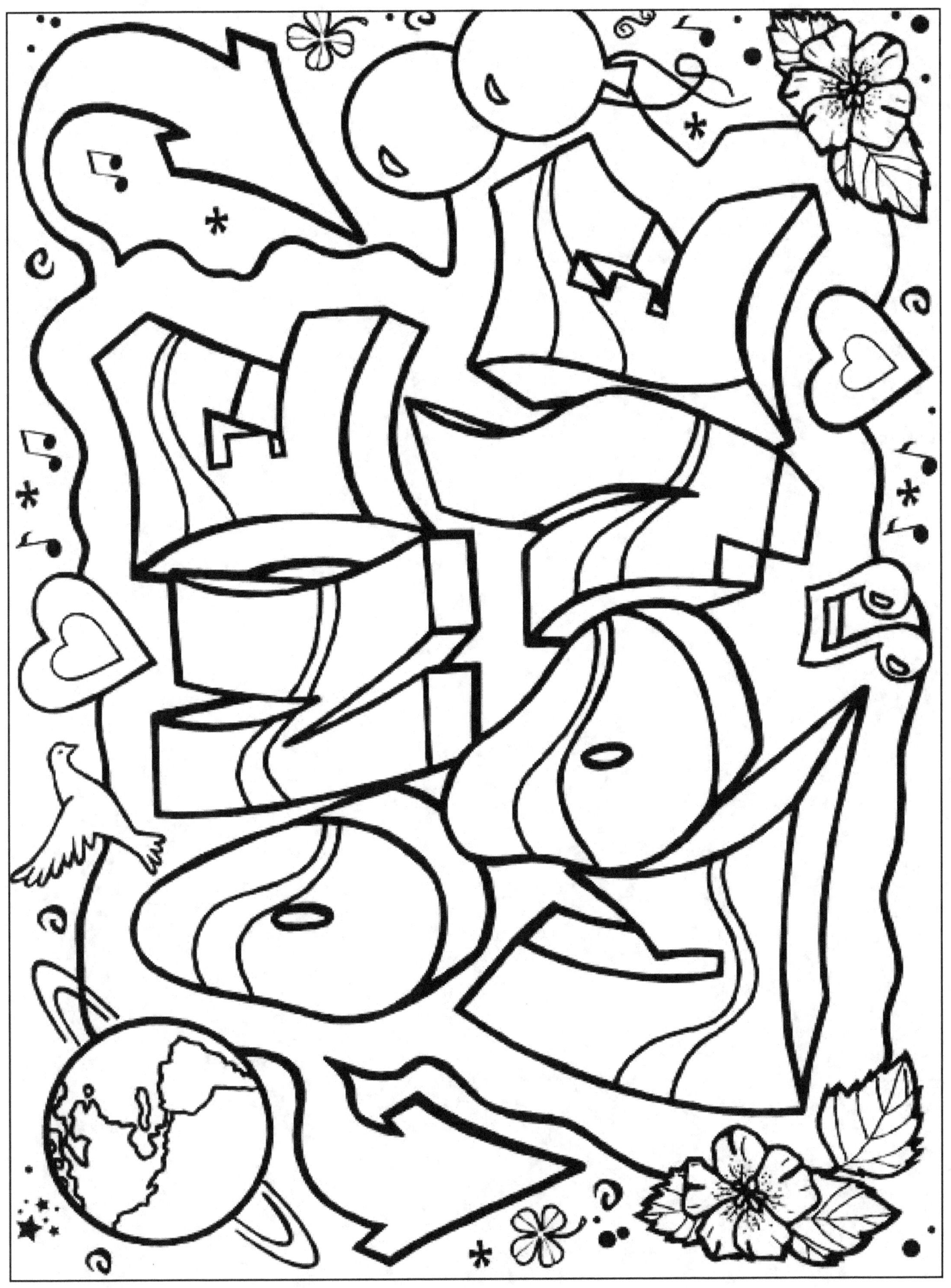

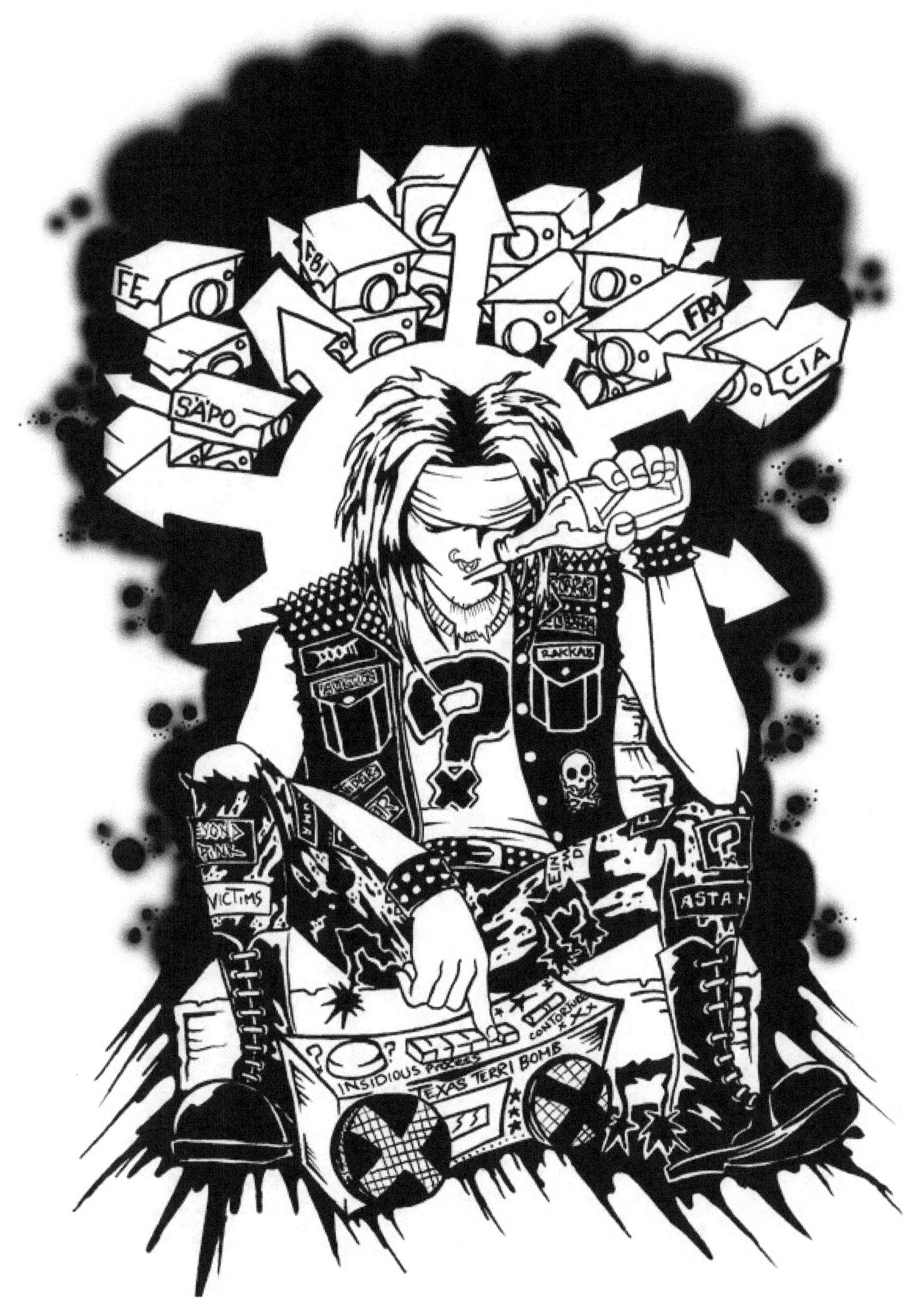

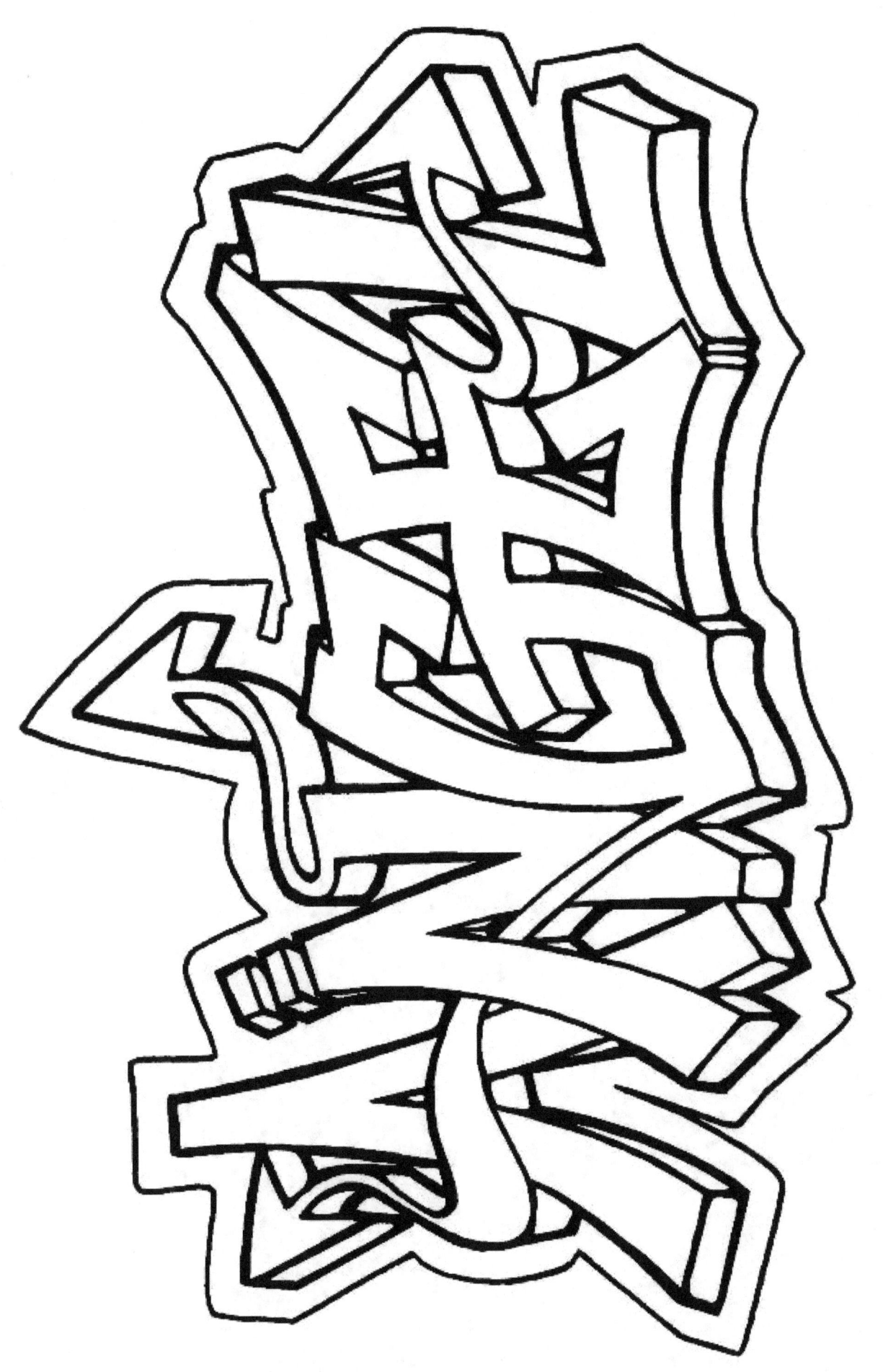

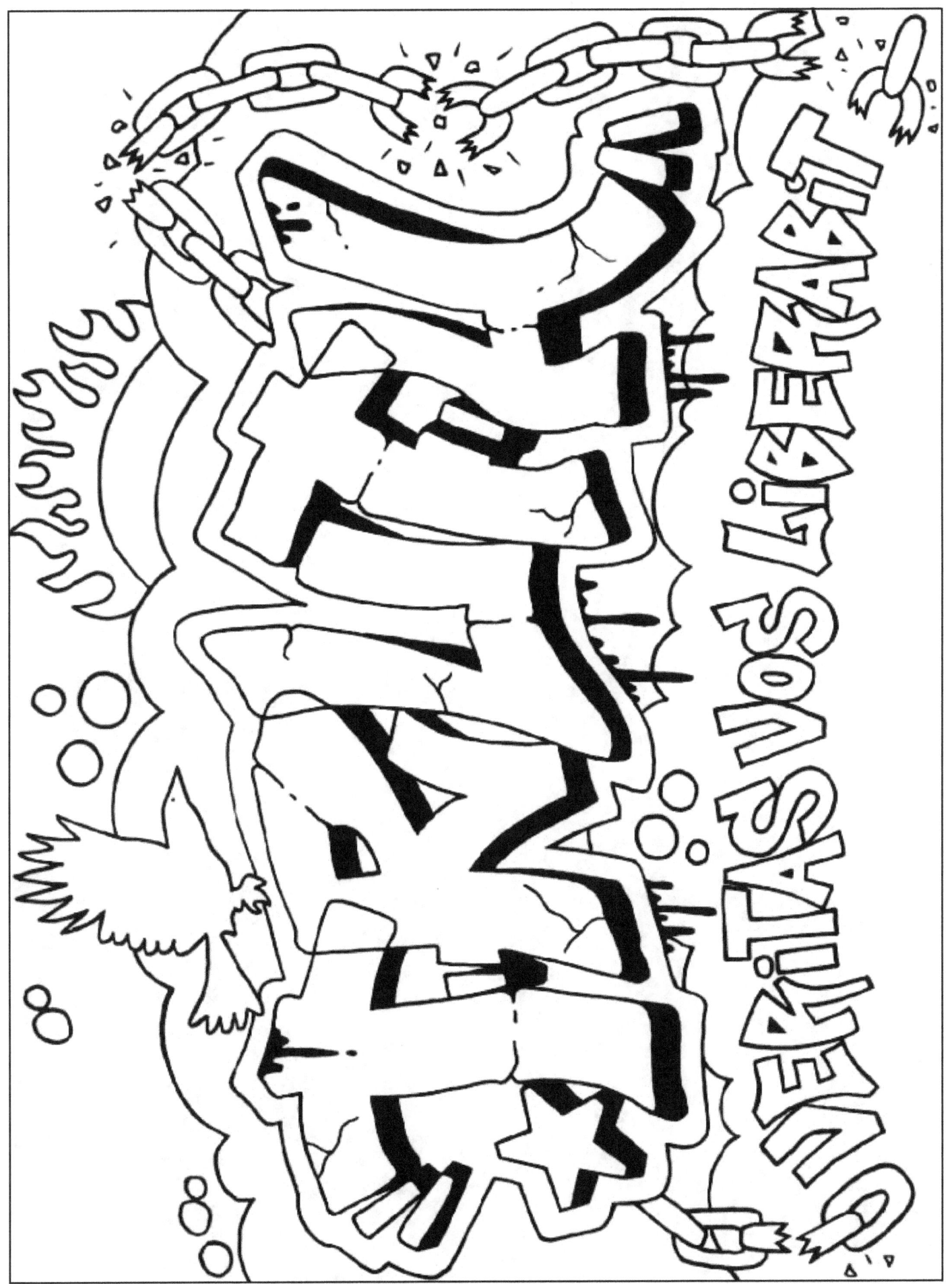

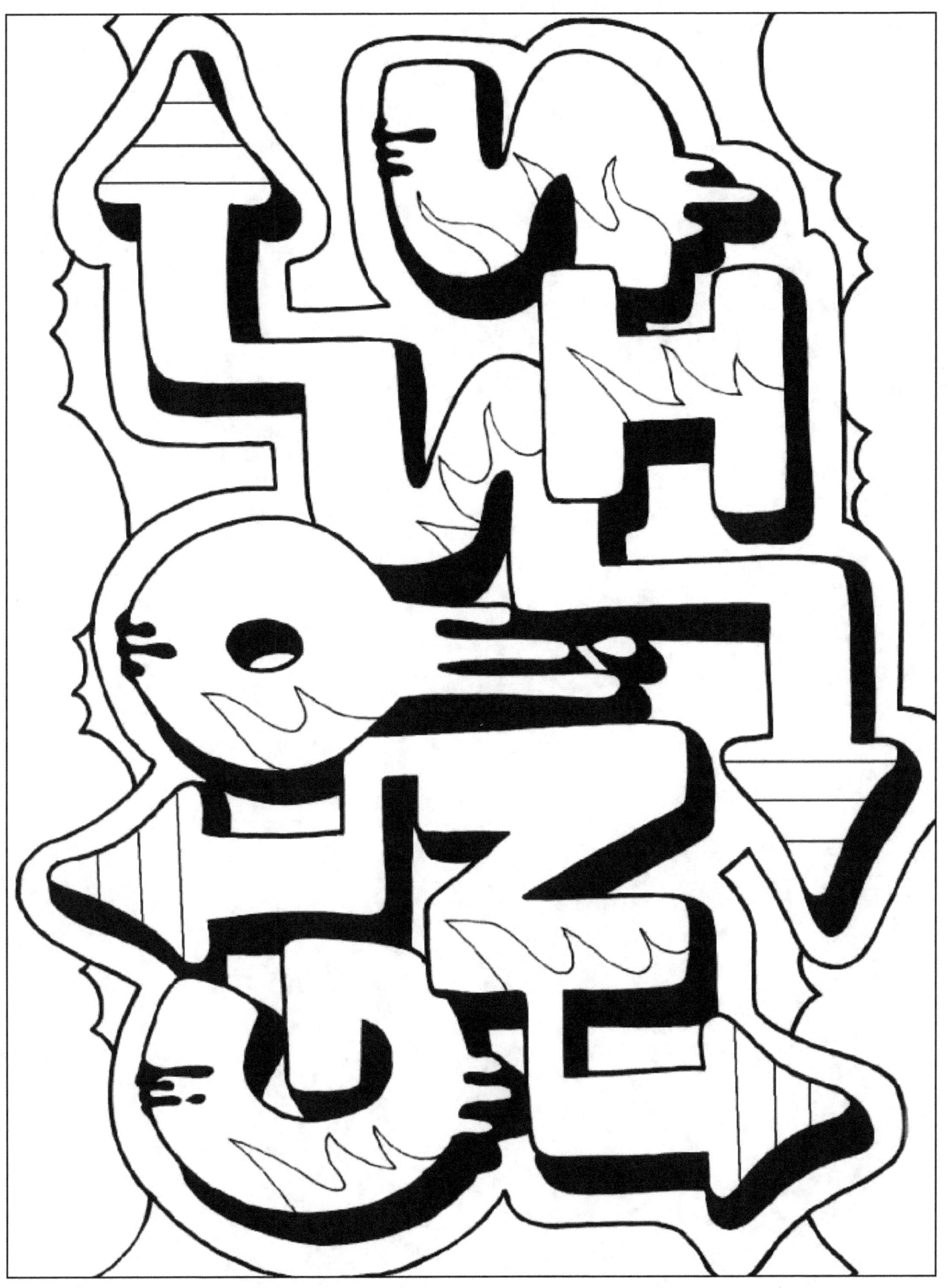

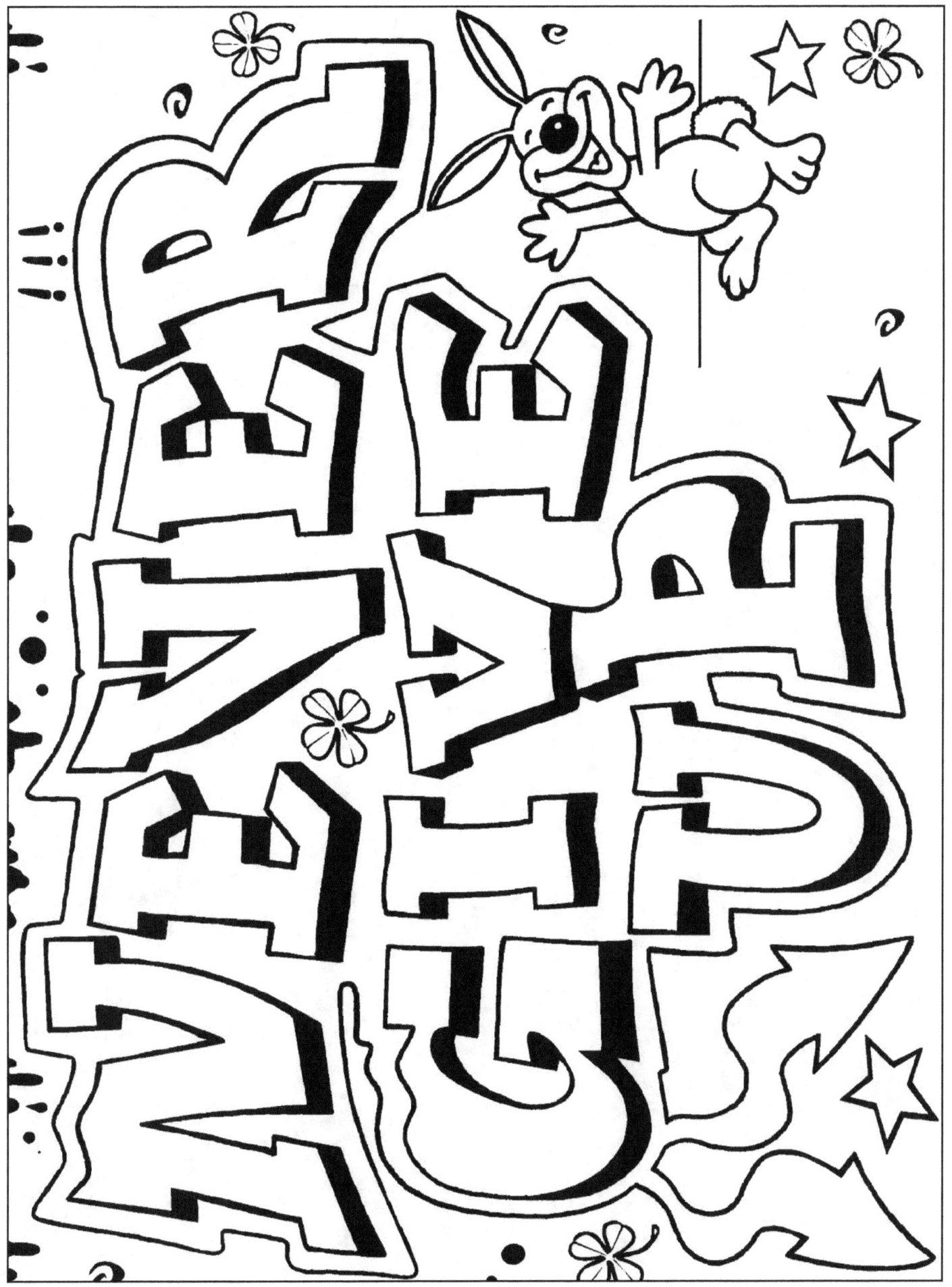

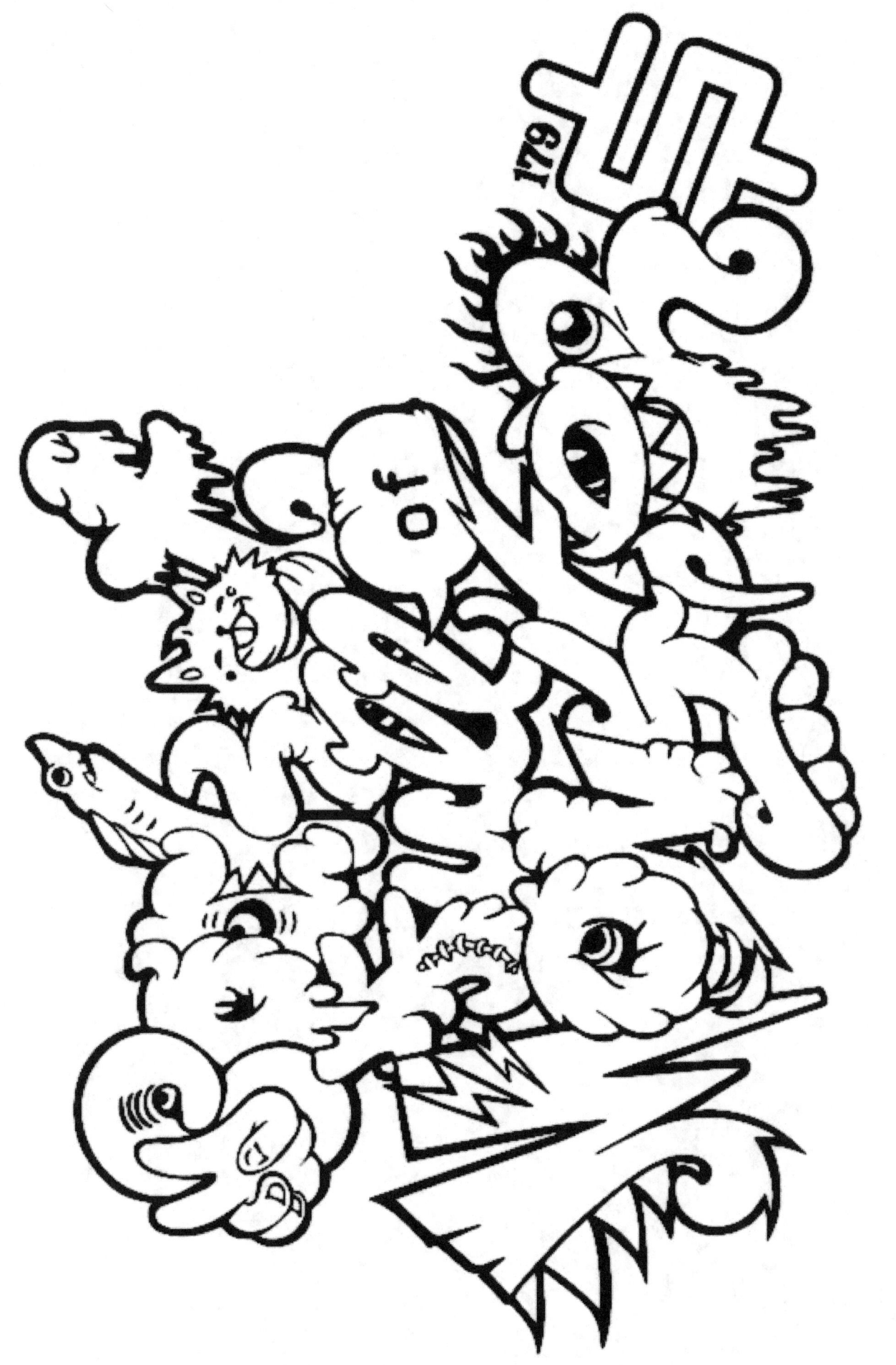

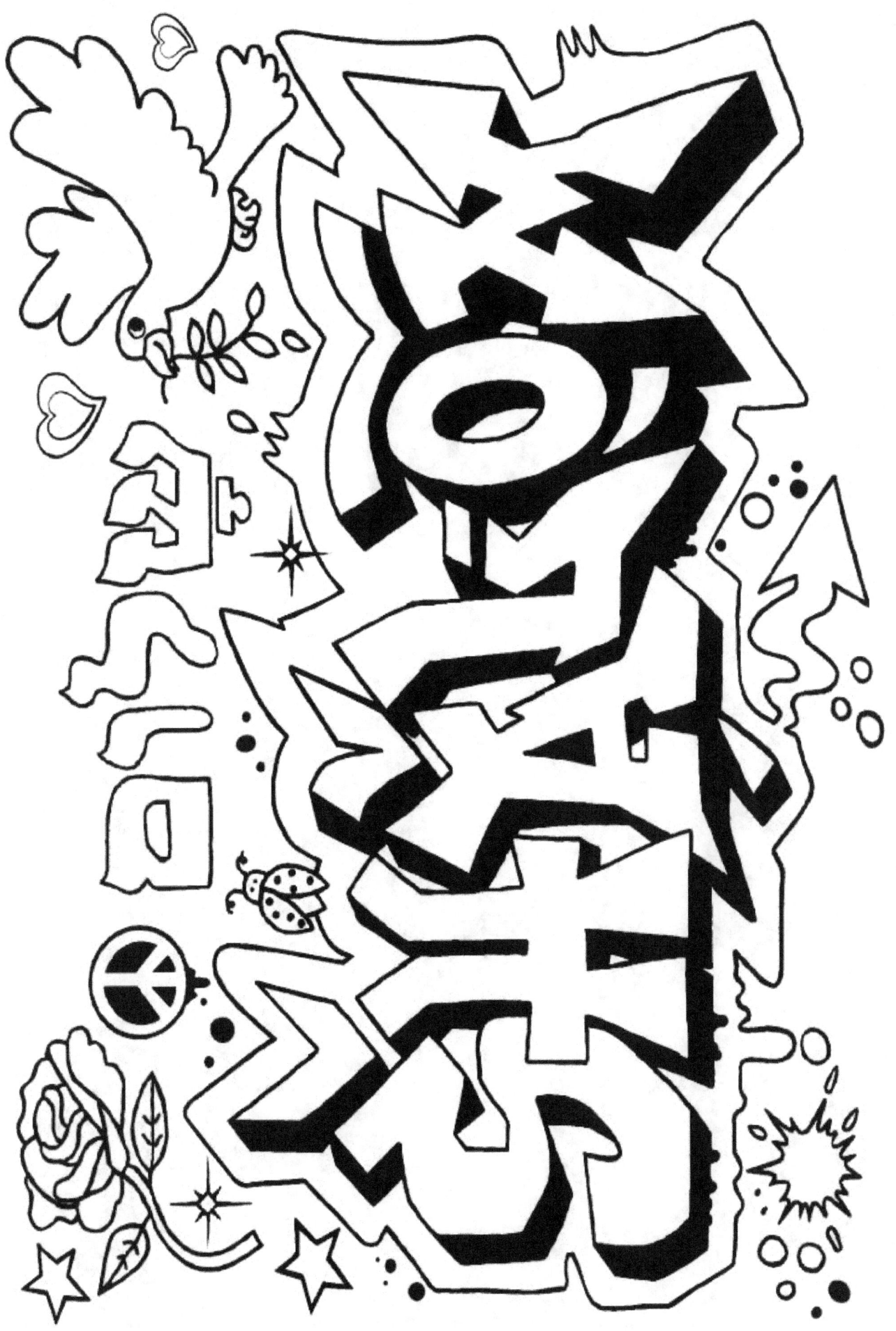

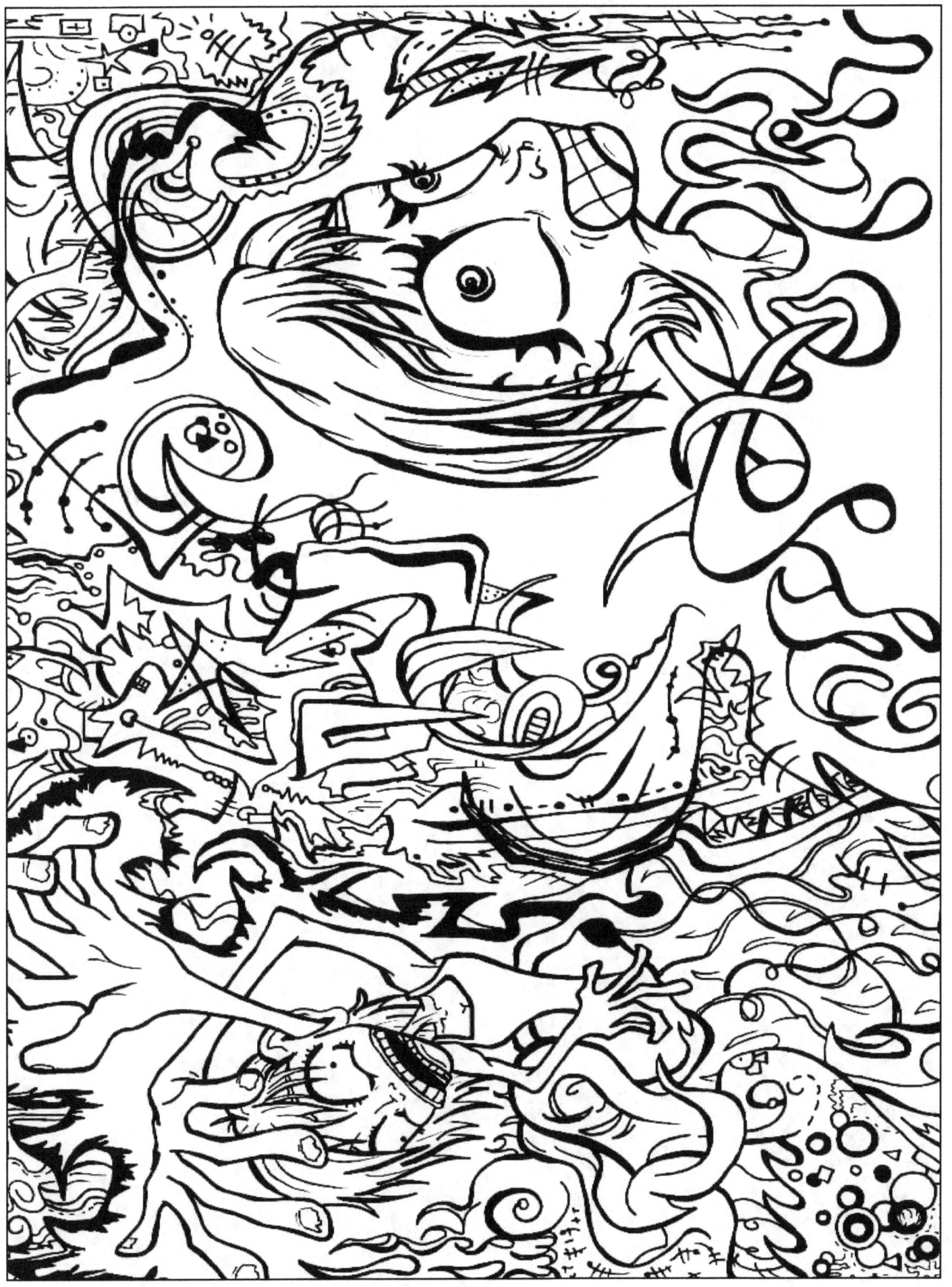

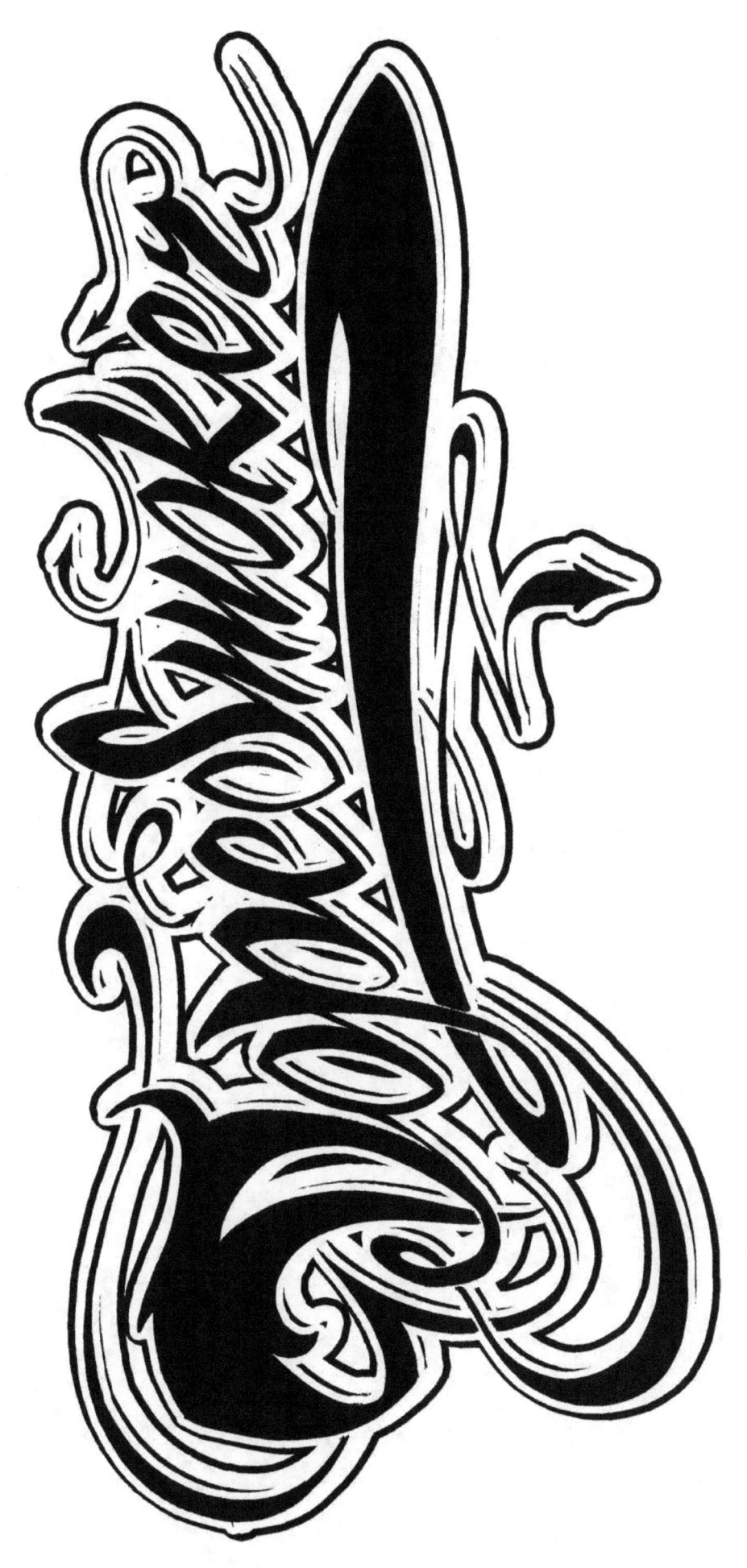

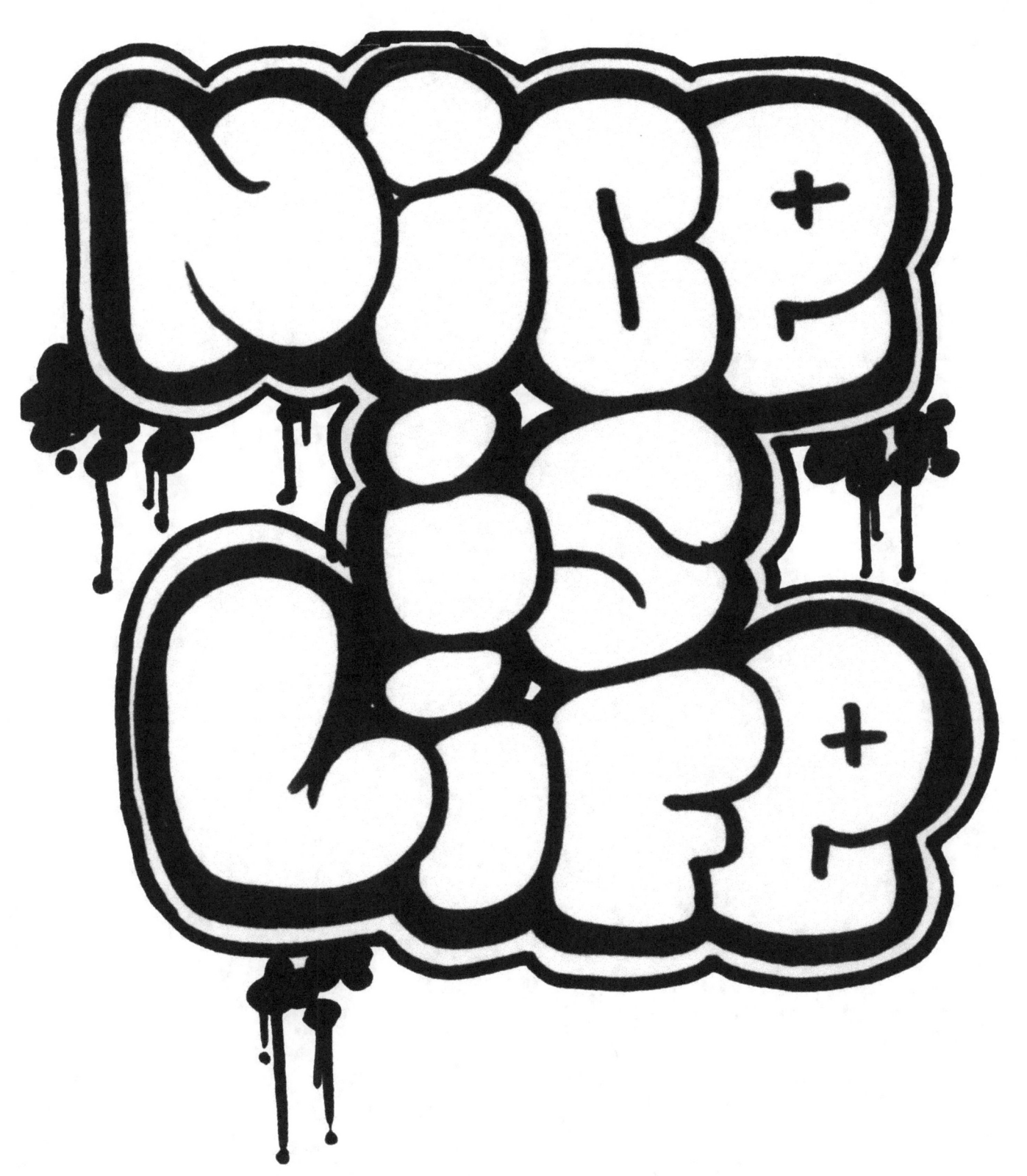

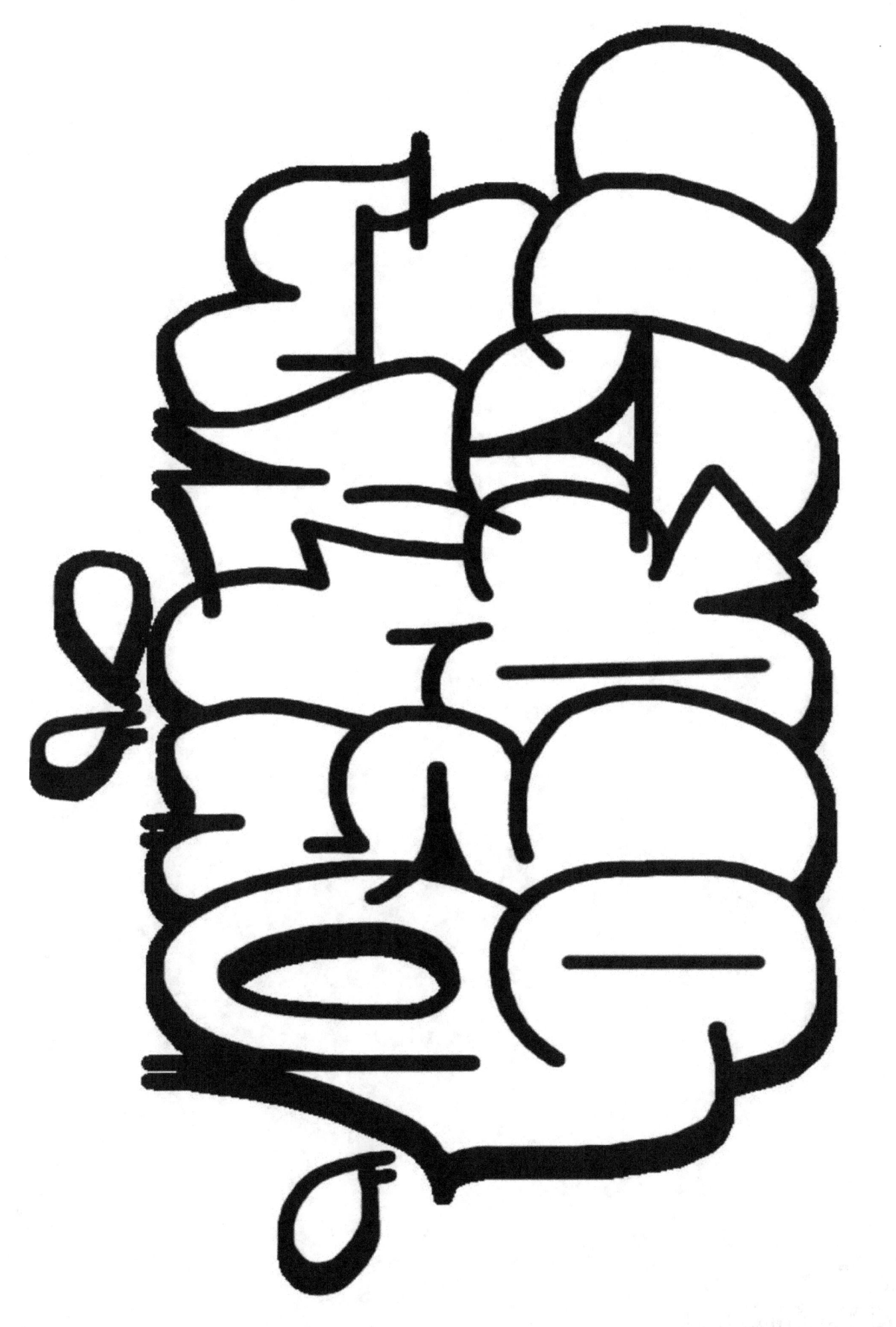

www.ingramcontent.com/pod-product-compliance
Lightning Source LLC
Chambersburg PA
CBHW080533220526
45465CB00006B/2687